AN

INTRODUCTION

TO THE

GREEK OF THE NEW TESTAMENT.

BY

GEO. L. CARY,

OF THE MEADVILLE THEOLOGICAL SCHOOL.

SECOND EDITION.

ANDOVER:

WARREN F. DRAPER,

MAIN STREET.

1881.

ELECTROTYPED AND PRINTED AT THE UNIVERSITY PRESS,
CAMBRIDGE.

PREFACE.

It is believed that there are many persons (some of them students in theology) unacquainted with the Greek language, and with neither time nor inclination for the study of classical Greek literature, who would nevertheless be glad to read the New Testament in its original tongue. For the aid of such, this little work has been prepared. It contains what is absolutely necessary for the understanding of New Testament Greek, omitting (or occasionally introducing in brackets) what is applicable only to classical authors. Not that a familiarity with this book alone will enable one to read offhand the Greek New Testament without further assistance ; but he who has faithfully studied this " Introduction" will then be in a situation to make use of more elaborate works. Perhaps the most helpful book to the beginner is "Bagster's Analytical Greek Lexicon," — too helpful if mental discipline is sought, but not if one's only aim is to economize time and labor. To the advanced student (supposed to be already in possession of some good New Testament Lexicon), Buttmann's "Grammar of the New Testament Greek " (or Winer's "Grammar of the Idiom of the New Testament ") is almost indispensable.

Notwithstanding the very elementary character of the following lessons, they presume in the learner an acquaintance with the fundamental principles of English grammar; only that which is peculiar to the Greek has been explained.

As very few inflected words occur in all their parts in the New Testament, different words have often been introduced into the same paradigm; therefore the student will probably find it best to memorize in order only the *terminations*. In the "Appendix" is a uniform paradigm of the regular verb, which will be found convenient for reference; also a tabular view of the endings of nouns.

Prior to publication, these lessons have been used with several classes in the "Meadville Theological School," and seem to have answered the purpose for which they were designed. Those familiar with them have been able to proceed at once (with the assistance above referred to) to the reading of the easier portions of the New Testament.

To Professor Ezra Abbot, of Harvard University, I am much indebted for assistance in the revision of proof-sheets and for valuable suggestions which have contributed to the completeness and accuracy of the work.

G. L. C.

MEADVILLE, PA., Dec. 1, 1878.

A SYNOPTIC TABLE OF CONTENTS.

ABBREVIATIONS.

A., acc. ...accusative.
act. ....active.
aor., A. ...aorist.
cf. ....*confer*, compare.
com. ......common.
D. ....dative.
e. g. ....*exempli gratia*, for example.
fem. ......feminine.
fut., F. ...future.
G. ....genitive.
indic. .....indicative.
imp. ......imperative.
imperf. ...imperfect.
inf. ....infinitive.
masc. .....masculine.
mid., m...middle.
MSS. ......manuscripts.
N. ....nominative.

neut. .....neuter.
N. T. .....New Testament.
opt. ....optative.
part. ......participle.
pass., p...passive.
perf., P...perfect.
pers. ......person.
pl. ....plural.
plup. ......pluperfect.
pres. ......present.
Rem. ......Remark, Remarks.
sing. ......singular.
subj. ......subjunctive.
Tisch......Tischendorf.
T. R. ......*textus receptus*, the received
           (Greek) text.
V. ....vocative.
v. ....verse.

INTRODUCTION.

1. THE GREEK ALPHABET.

Characters.		Names.	English Equivalents.
A	a	Alpha	a
B	β	Bēta	b
Γ	γ	Gamma	g
Δ	δ	Dĕlta	d
E	ϵ	Epsilón	ĕ
Z	ζ	Zēta	z
H	η	Eta	ē
Θ	θ	Thēta	th
I	ι	Iŏta	i
K	κ	Kappa	k
Λ	λ	Lambda	l
M	μ	Mu	m
N	ν	Nu	n
Ξ	ξ	Xi	x
O	o	Omicrón	ŏ
Π	π	Pi	p
P	ρ	Rho	r
Σ	σ, ς	Sigma	s
T	τ	Tau	t
Υ	υ	Upsilón	u
Φ	ϕ	Phi	ph
X	χ	Chi	ch
Ψ	ψ	Psi	ps
Ω	ω	Omĕga	ō

Rem. a. When ι is written under another vowel, thus, ᾳ, it is called *iota subscript.*

Rem. b. Most editors use the character ς at the end of words, instead of σ.

2. PRONUNCIATION.

Rem. a. Although there is a lack of agreement among scholars as to the best pronunciation of Greek, the tendency in this country is decidedly towards the adoption of what is called the "Continental" method, the essential features of which are presented in the following *Remarks.*

Rem. b. α has the sound of *a* in *father.* At the end of an unaccented syllable * it is usually obscure, like the *a* in *penalty*, except at the end of a word. Before consonants in the same syllable it is usually short, like *a* in *hat.* The diphthong αι is pronounced like *ai* in *aisle*, and αυ like *ou* in *house.*

Rem. c. γ is always hard, like *g* in *give.* Before κ, γ, χ, ξ, it has the sound of *ng.*

Rem. d. ε is pronounced like *e* in *get*, ει like *ei* in *height.*

Rem. e. η is pronounced like *a* in *fate.*

Rem. f. θ has the sound of *th* in *thin.*

Rem. g. ι has the sound of *i* in *machine*, except before a consonant in the same syllable, where it is pronounced like *i* in *pin.*

Rem. h. ξ has the force of *ks.*

Rem. i. ο is usually sounded like *o* in *not*, but at the end of a syllable it approximates to the *o* in *note.* The diphthong ου has the sound of *oo* in *moon ;* οι does not differ from the English *oi.*

Rem. j. υ and ευ are to be sounded like *ew* in *few*, υι like *we.*

Rem. k. Few persons distinguish in pronunciation between χ

---

* Syllables are divided, as far as possible, according to English analogy.

and κ, but it is better to give χ the sound of the German *ch* (as it is pronounced after *a*, *o*, *u*) and the Spanish *j*.

Rem. l. ω has the sound of *o* in *note*.

Rem. m. The diphthongs ᾳ, ῃ, ῳ (for ᾳ, ῃ, ῳ) are pronounced like *a*, *η*, *ω*.

Rem. n. The names of the letters of the alphabet (given on page 1) are to be pronounced according to the foregoing rules.

3. PUNCTUATION, BREATHINGS, AND ACCENTS.

Rem. a. The marks of punctuation peculiar to the Greek are the colon [·] and the mark of interrogation [;].

Rem. b. The rough breathing ['] before or above a vowel at the beginning of a word has the force of *h*; the smooth breathing ['] only indicates the absence of aspiration.

Rem. c. The breathings are also used, in certain cases, with the consonant ρ; but no distinction is now made, in pronunciation, between ῥ and ῥ.

Rem. d. The accents [' *acute*, ' *grave*, ^ *circumflex*] indicate on what syllables the stress of voice is to be laid. The *grave* accent is found only on *final* syllables, where it regularly takes the place of the acute *in continued discourse*, and indicates that the syllable, *while the word stands in that position*, has a softened tone.

Rem. e. Very few of these marks of discrimination are found in the older manuscripts. Modern editors punctuate according to their own judgment.

4. CLASSIFICATION OF THE CONSONANTS.

Rem. a. The consonants are divided, with reference to the organs chiefly concerned in their production, into *labials* (π, β, φ, μ), *linguals* (τ, δ, θ, ζ, σ, λ, ν, ρ), and *palatals* (κ, γ, χ). The *double consonants,* ξ and ψ, are virtually included in this classification, being equivalent respectively to κσ and πσ.

Rem. b. λ, μ, ν, ρ, are also called *liquids.*

Rem. c. The *mutes* are divided into *smooth* (π, κ, τ), *middle* (β, γ, δ), and *rough* (φ, χ, θ). Those produced by the same organs (for instance the labials π, β, φ) are called *cognate.*

I.

§ 1. A verb ending in ω,* in the present, indicative, active.

πιστεύω, *I believe.* (Mark ix. 24.)
πιστεύεις, *thou believest.* (Acts xxvi. 27.)
πιστεύει, *he believes.* (John xii. 44.)†
πιστεύομεν, *we believe.* (John iv. 42.)
πιστεύετε, *you believe.* (John iii. 12.)
πιστεύουσι(ν), *they believe.* (John xvi. 9.)

Rem. a. The present tense, in all its modes, represents an action or state as *continued or repeated.*

Rem. b. The unchangeable part of an inflected word (for example, πιστευ in the verb πιστεύω) is called the *stem.*

Rem. c. The terminations appended to the stems of verbs indicate the person and number of the subject.

Rem. d. Verbs in the third person ending in σι and ε (with a few exceptions) may drop the ν before a consonant.

§ 2. The personal pronouns, in the nominative case.‡

ἐγὼ ἔχω, *I have.* (Matt. iii. 14.)
σὺ ἔχεις, *thou hast.* (Rom. xiv. 22.) §
ἡμεῖς ἔχομεν, *we have.* (John. xix. 7.)
ὑμεῖς ἔχετε, *you have.* (John xvi. 22.)

Rem. A personal pronoun, when expressed as the subject of a verb, is usually, if not always, emphatic.

---

* Most Greek verbs end in ω in the first pers. sing. of the pres. ind. act.

† In the third pers. sing., when the subject of the verb is not expressed, we must determine from the context whether *he, she,* or *it* is to be supplied in translation.

‡ See § 63.

§ The context alone can determine whether a verb in the ind. mode is declarative or interrogative. In the present passage, the T. R. punctuates interrogatively.

TRANSLATE *

1. λέγω. (Matt. xxvi. 64.) 2. λέγει. (Matt. xxvi. 38.) 3. λέγομεν. (Rom. iv. 9.) 4. λέγεις. (Matt. xxvi. 70.) 5. λέγουσι. (Matt. xi. 18.) 6. λέγετε. (Matt. xvi. 2.) 7. καὶ λέγει. (Matt. iv. 6.) 8. ἐγὼ δὲ λέγω. (Matt. v. 32.) 9. ἔχετε; (Matt. v. 46.) 10. ἔχετε. (Matt. vi. 8.)

II.

§ 3. Verbs in -ω, in the imperfect, indicative, active.

ἔλεγον,† *I said,* or *was saying.* (2 Thess. ii. 5.)
εἶχες, *thou hadst.* (John xix. 11.)‡
ἐπίστευεν, [*he*]§ *trusted.* (John ii. 24.) *
εἴχομεν, *we had.* (Heb. xii. 9.)
ἐπιστεύετε, *you believed.* (John v. 46.)
ἐπίστευον, *they believed.* (John xii. 37.)

Rem. a. The imperfect tense represents an action or state as *continued or repeated* in past time, and may often be rendered into English by *was* and the present participle. In conditional sentences it may refer to present time: *e. g.* εἰ γὰρ ἐπιστεύετε Μωϋσεῖ, ἐπιστεύετε ἂν ἐμοί, *for if you believed Moses, you would believe me.* (John v. 46.)

Rem. b. The imperfect tense sometimes has a *conative* force, indicating only the *attempt* to perform an action. Thus in Acts vii. 26, συνήλλασσεν αὐτοὺς εἰς εἰρήνην is to be rendered *he endeavored to reconcile them* and not *he reconciled* or *was reconciling them.* Even the present tense occasionally has this conative force : *e. g.* λιθάζετε, John x. 32.

---

* For the meanings of words not already defined, see the "Vocabulary" at the end of the book. In accordance with the general custom, the Greek verbs are there given in the first pers. of the pres. ind., and their English equivalents in the infinitive.

† Whenever, in Lessons II.-XXXIII., other verbs are substituted for πιστεύω as examples of the inflection of verbs in -ω, the learner is to understand that the corresponding forms of πιστεύω are not found in the N. T.

‡ The second pers. sing. and the first pers. pl. of the imperf. ind. act. are of exceedingly rare occurrence in the N. T. Tischendorf's text has ἔχεις in this passage.

§ Pronouns in brackets represent subjects which are expressed in the context. For example, in the present passage, the text says Ἰησοῦς ἐπίστευεν, *Jesus trusted.*

Rem. c. The vowel ε (rarely η), prefixed in certain past tenses to verbs beginning with a consonant, is called the *syllabic augment*. In verbs beginning with ρ, the ρ is usually doubled after the augment. The few exceptions to the doubling of the ρ all occur in other tenses than the imperfect, and but a single case is found outside the epistles.

Rem. d. Verbs beginning with a vowel usually have (in the tenses above referred to) a *temporal augment*, obtained by lengthening the vowel, α and ε becoming η (ε sometimes ει) and ο becoming ω. Thus ἀκούω becomes in the imperf. ἤκουον.

TRANSLATE

1. ἔλεγεν.[1] (Matt. ix. 21.) 2. εἴχετε. (1 John ii. 7.) 3. ἔλεγον.[2] (Matt. xxvi. 5.) 4. νῦν δὲ λέγετε. (John ix. 41.) 5. σὺ πιστεύεις; (John ix. 35.) 6. ἐδίδασκεν. (Matt. v. 2.) 7. ἐκήρυσσεν. (Acts ix. 20.) 8. δουλεύω. (Luke xv. 29.) 9. δουλεύει.[1] (Gal. iv. 25.) 10. ἀκούετε. (Matt. x. 27.)

[1] The context shows the gender of the subject to be feminine.
[2] The subject is plural.

III.

§ 4. Verbs in -ω, in the future, indicative, active.

πιστεύσω, *I shall*, or *will, believe.* (John xx. 25.)
λατρεύσας, *thou shalt serve.* (Matt. iv. 10).
τίς πιστεύσει; *who will intrust?* (Luke xvi. 11.)
πιστεύσομεν,* *we will believe.* (Matt. xxvii. 42.)
πιστεύσετε; *will you believe?* (John iii. 12.)
πιστεύσουσιν, [*they*] *will believe.* (John xi. 48.)

Rem. a. The consonant which, in several tenses, stands between the stem and the personal vowel-endings, is called the *tense characteristic*. It is not found in all verbs.

ἕξεις, *thou shalt*, or *wilt, have.* (Matt. xix. 21.)
γράψω, *I will write.* (Rev. iii. 12.)

Rem. b. The double consonant ξ may originate in any of the three

---

* This is the reading of the T. R., from which Tisch. differs.

combinations, κσ, γσ, χσ; the double consonant ψ, in πσ, βσ, φσ. Thus ἕχσεις becomes ἕξεις, and γράφσω becomes γράψω.

Rem. c. The aspiration of the ε in the future of ἕχω is merely a relic of the σ with which the root of the verb once commenced.

τηρήσω, *I shall, or will, keep.* (2 Cor. xi. 9.)

Rem. d. When the last letter of the root of a verb is a short vowel, it is usually lengthened in all tenses except the present and the imperfect. Thus from τηρέω we have the future τηρήσω.

TRANSLATE

1. βασιλεύσει. (Luke i. 33.) 2. ἀκούσετε. (Matt. xiii. 14.) 3. ἀκούσουσιν. (John x. 16.) 4. λατρεύσουσιν. (Acts vii. 7.) 5. βασιλεύσουσιν. (Rev. xx. 6.) 6. πῶς δὲ πιστεύσουσιν; (Rom. x. 14.) 7. ἐτρέχετε καλῶς. (Gal. v. 7.) 8. τηρήσει. (John xiv. 23.) 9. λατρεύουσιν. (Rev. vii. 15.) 10. ἐγὼ τρέχω. (1 Cor. ix. 26.)

IV.

§ 5. A verb in -ω, in the aorist, indicative, active.

ἐπίστευσα, *I believed.* (2 Cor. iv. 13.)

ἐπίστευσας, *thou believedst.* (Matt. viii. 13.)

ἐπίστευσεν, *he believed.* (John iv. 53.)

ἐπιστεύσαμεν, *we believed,* or *became believers.* (Rom. xiii. 11.)

ἐπιστεύσατε, *you believed.* (Matt. xxi. 32.)

ἐπίστευσαν, *they believed.* (John ii. 22.)

Rem. a. The aorist *indicative* denotes simply *the past occurrence* of an action or state; but it sometimes has the force of the English perfect or pluperfect. In the *dependent modes*, except in indirect discourse, the distinction of *time* between the present and the aorist disappears.

Rem. b. The imperfect and aorist tenses are the only ones which regularly take the *augment*.

§ 6. Nouns, with the article, in the nominative singular.

ὁ πατὴρ ἔλεγεν, *the father said.* (Mark ix. 24.)

λέγει ἡ μήτηρ, *the mother says.* (John ii. 3.)

ἔλαμψεν τὸ πρόσωπον, *the face shone.* (Matt. xvii. 2.)

Rem. The article is inflected to indicate gender, number, and case, and must agree in these respects with the noun which it limits. The form ὁ is masculine, ἡ feminine, and τό neuter.*

TRANSLATE

1. ἤκουσας. (John xi. 41.) 2. ἤκουσα. (John viii. 40.) 3. ἠκού-
σαμεν. (Luke xxii. 71.) 4. ἤκουσαν. (Luke ii. 20.) 5. ἤκουσεν.
(Luke xv. 25.) 6. ἠκούσατε. (Matt. xxvi. 65.) 7. ἔγραψα. (Rom.
xv. 15.) 8. ἔγραψεν. (Mark x. 5.) 9. ἐγράψατε. (1 Cor. vii. 1.)
10. λάμπει. (Matt. v. 15.)

V.

§ 7. Verbs in -ω, in the perfect, indicative, active.

πεπίστευκα, *I have believed,* or *put trust in.* (2 Tim. i. 12.)
πεπίστευκας, *thou hast believed.* (John xx. 29.)
πεπίστευκεν, *he has believed.* (John iii. 18.)
ἡμεῖς πεπιστεύκαμεν, *we have believed.* (John vi. 69.)
ὑμεῖς πεπιστεύκατε, *you have believed.* (John xvi. 27.)
τετηρήκασι(ν), *they have kept.* (John xvii. 6.)

Rem. a. The termination of the third person plural is sometimes αν
instead of ασι(ν).

Rem. b. In the perfect and pluperfect tenses, whenever the root begins with a consonant (other than ρ, ζ, ξ, ψ) followed by a vowel or a
liquid, a special kind of augment called the *reduplication* is generally
prefixed to the root. This consists of the first letter of the verb (or, if
this is a rough mute, its corresponding smooth) followed by ε. In other
cases, these tenses simply take the usual augment. There are one or two
instances, though not in the T. R., of reduplication in verbs beginning
with ρ.

§ 8. Nouns of the first declension, in the nominative sin-
gular.

ἡ δόξα καὶ ἡ σοφία καὶ ἡ τιμή, *glory and wisdom and honor.* (Rev. vii. 12.)

---

* In the Vocabulary, the gender of nouns is indicated by the article placed
after them.

Ἠλείας,* *Elias*, or *Elijah.* (Matt. xi. 14.)
Ἰούδας, *Judas.* (Mark xiv. 10.)
ὁ δεσπότης, *Master !* or *Lord !* (Rev. vi. 10.)

Rem. a. Greek nouns are classed together, according to similarity of inflection, into three *declensions.*

Rem. b. Nouns of the first declension are either masculine, ending in as or ης, or feminine, ending in a or η.

Rem. c. In the N. T., nouns in as of the first declension are, with one or two exceptions, proper names.

Rem. d. Abstract nouns and nominatives used in address often take the article, which must, of course, be omitted in translation.

TRANSLATE

1. τετήρηκα. (John xv. 10.) · 2. λαλήσω. (John xiv. 30.) 3. λελάληκα. (John xiv. 25.) 4. ἐλάλησα. (2 Cor. iv. 13.) 5. καὶ ἐβασίλευσαν. (Rev. xx. 4.) 6. δεδουλεύκαμεν. (John viii. 33.) 7. ἐδούλευσεν. (Phil. ii. 22.) 8. ἐδουλεύσατε. (Gal. iv. 8.) 9. ἐβασίλευσας. (Rev. xi. 17.) 10. Ἡσαίας ὁ προφήτης. (John i. 23.)

VI.

§ 9. Verbs in -ω, in the pluperfect, indicative, active.

ᾔδειν,† *I knew.* (John i. 31.)
ᾔδας,† *thou knewest.* (Matt. xxv. 26.)
ὃς περιπεπατήκει, *who had walked.* (Acts xiv. 8.)‡
[ἐβεβουλεύκειμεν, *we had advised.*]
ᾔδατε ;† *knew ye ?* (Luke ii. 49.)
πεπιστεύκεισαν, *they had believed.* (Acts xiv. 23.)

Rem. a. The augment of a verb is seldom and the reduplication never affected by prefixing a preposition to the verb.

Rem. b. In classical Greek, the pluperfect tense usually takes, if possible, the syllabic augment in addition to the reduplication; but in

---

* In the T. R. Ἠλίας.

† From the irregular verb εἴδω, whose pluperfect has the force of an imperfect. See § 46, *Rem. b.*

‡ Tisch. reads περιεπάτησεν.

N. T. Greek this is rare. In Acts xiv. 8, the Elzevir text reads περιεπατήκει.

Rem. c. Verbs whose roots end in a smooth or middle labial or palatal (see p. 3, 4, *Rem. a*) have the *rough breathing* instead of κ for the tense characteristic of the perfect and pluperfect tenses, the consonant combining with the breathing to form the corresponding rough mute.

§ 10. Nouns of the first declension, in the genitive singular, with and without the article.

τῆς δόξης, *of glory.* (Acts vii. 2.)
σοφίας, *of wisdom.* (Acts. vi. 3.)
τιμῆς, *of honor.* (1 Tim. v. 17.)
Ἠλείου, *of Elias.* (Luke iv. 25.) *
Ἰούδα, *of Judas.* (Mark vi. 3.)
τοῦ προφήτου, *of the prophet.* (Luke iii. 4.)

Rem. a. In translating the genitive case, we are frequently obliged to supply certain prepositions, particularly *of.* This circumlocution may often be avoided by the use of the possessive case, to which the genitive in many respects corresponds.

Rem. b. Nouns of the first declension ending in a vowel commonly have their genitive in -ης; but those in -α pure (*i. e.* -α preceded by a vowel), and usually those in -ρα, retain the α throughout the singular number. So also does μνᾶ, contracted from μνάα.

Rem. c. Nouns of the first declension in -ας not pure form the genitive in -α. Some proper names in -ης have their genitive in -η, but these were not originally Greek words.

Rem. d. Contrary to the rule (*Rem. b*) Μάρθα has for its genitive Μάρθας, and, in some of the best MSS., the genitive of Λύδδα is Λύδδας; but these nouns are from the Hebrew. See § 43.

TRANSLATE

1. ἐβασίλευσεν ἡ ἁμαρτία. (Rom. v. 21.) 2. ἡ ἀγάπη οὐδέποτε ἐκπίπτει. (1 Cor. xiii. 8.) 3. Ἡσαίας λέγει. (Rom. xv. 12.) 4. ἤκουσεν Ἡρώδης ὁ τετράρχης. (Matt. xiv. 1.) 5. τῆς ἁμαρτίας. (John viii. 34.) 6. τῆς ἀγάπης. (2 Cor. xiii. 11.) 7. Ἡρώδου τοῦ τετράρχου. (Acts xiii. 1.) 8. γῆ Ἰούδα.† (Matt. ii. 6.) 9. ὁ πατὴρ τῆς δόξης. (Eph. i. 17.) 10. μετὰ δόξης. (2 Tim. ii. 10.)

* In Luke i. 17 (the only other passage where this word is found in the gen.), Tisch. reads Ἠλεία.
† See Vocabulary.

VII.

§ 11. Verbs in -ω, in the present, subjunctive, active.

τί λέγω; *what shall I say?* or, *why should I say?* (Heb. xi. 32.)

ἐὰν * προσφέρῃς, *if thou bringest.* (Matt. v. 23.)

ὃς ἂν * πιστεύῃ, *whoever shall believe.* (Mark xi. 23.)

ἵνα λέγωμεν, *that we say,* or, *to say.* (2 Cor. ix. 4.)

κἂν * πιστεύητε, *even if,* or *though, you believe.* (John x. 38.) †

ὅταν * λέγωσιν, *when they say, are saying,* or *shall say.* (1 Thess. v. 3.)

Rem. a. Actions and states expressed in the subjunctive mode are simply *conceived* of as *possible,* not affirmed to be real.

Rem. b. In some respects, this mode corresponds to the English potential and subjunctive modes ; yet it must very often be translated by the indicative, infinitive, or imperative.

Rem. c. In the various tenses of the subjunctive mode, the element of *time* is subordinate to that of *manner,* and, in dependent sentences, is determined by the time of the leading verb. Cf. § 1, *Rem. a.*

§ 12. Nouns of the first declension, in the dative singular, with and without the article.

δόξῃ καὶ τιμῇ, *with glory and honor.* (Heb. ii. 7.)

ἐν τῇ σοφίᾳ, *in wisdom.* (Luke ii. 52.)

'Ηλείᾳ, *for Elias.* (Matt. xvii. 4.)

'Ιούδᾳ, *to Judas.* (John xiii. 26.)

τῷ δεσπότῃ, *to,* or *for, the master.* (2 Tim. ii. 21.)

Rem. a. In translating the dative case, we must often supply prepositions, particularly *to, for,* and *with.*

Rem. b. In some MSS. 'Ιωάννει is found, instead of 'Ιωάννῃ, as the dative of 'Ιωάννης.

TRANSLATE

1. ἐβασιλεύσατε. (1 Cor. iv. 8.)   2. ἵνα μὴ λέγω. (Phil. 19.)   3. ὅταν λέγῃ τις.[1] (1 Cor. iii. 4.)   4. ἵνα λέγητε. (1 Cor. i. 10.)   5. ἔχωμεν.[2] (Heb. xii. 28.)   6. λατρεύωμεν.[3] (Heb. xii. 28.)   7. ἐὰν ἔχητε. (Matt.

---

* See Vocabulary.

† Tisch. reads πιστεύετε.

xvii. 20.) 8. ὃς ἂν μὴ ἔχῃ. (Luke viii. 18.) 9. ἵνα ἔχητε. (John v. 40.)
10. ἵνα ἔχωσιν. (John x. 10.)

¹ Notice the difference in accent and position between τίς interrogative and τις indefinite. The latter never stands at the beginning of a sentence.
² The first person of the subjunctive is often used in exhortations.
³ The context shows that this should be translated by the potential mode, using the auxiliary *may.*

VIII.

§13. A verb in -ω, in the aorist, subjunctive, active.

ἵνα πιστεύσω, *that I may believe.* (John ix. 36.)
ἐὰν πιστεύσῃς, *if thou believest.* (John xi. 40.)
ἵνα πιστεύσῃ, *that* [*it*] *may believe.* (John xvii. 21.)
ἵνα πιστεύσωμεν, *that we may believe.* (Mark xv. 32.)
μὴ πιστεύσητε, *believe not.* (Matt. xxiv. 23.)
ἵνα πιστεύσωσιν, *that they might believe.* (John xi. 42.)

Rem. On the aorist subjunctive, see §5, *Rem. a,* and §11, *Rem. a, b, c.*

§14. Nouns of the first declension, in the accusative singular, with and without the article.

δόξαν καὶ τιμήν, *glory and honor.* (Rev. iv. 9.)
τὴν σοφίαν, *the wisdom.* (Luke xi. 31.)
Ἡλείαν, *Elias.* (Matt. xvi. 14.)
Ἰούδαν, *Judas.* (Mark iii. 19.)
τὸν δεσπότην, *the master.* (Jude 4.)

Rem. The Greek accusative case does not differ essentially in its uses from the English objective.

§15. Nouns of the first declension, in the vocative singular.

Ἰούδα, *Judas!* (Luke xxii. 48.)
δέσποτα, *Master!* or *Lord!* (Luke ii. 29.)

Rem. The vocative case is used in exclamation and address. In the plural number, and sometimes in the singular, the nominative form is used for the vocative.

TRANSLATE

1. οὐ μὴ πιστεύσητε.¹ (Luke xxii. 67.) 2. ἵνα πιστεύσητε. (John xi. 15.) 3. ἐὰν γὰρ μὴ πιστεύσητε. (John viii. 24.) 4. μεμίσηκεν. (John xv. 18.) 5. μεμισήκασιν. (John xv. 24.) 6. δόξαν οὐ λαμβάνω.

(John v. 41.) 7. καὶ οὐ λαμβάνετε. (John v. 43.) 8. ἀπὸ δόξης εἰς δόξαν. (2 Cor. iii. 18.) 9. Ἰησοῦς * ἐμαρτύρησεν ὅτι προφήτης τιμὴν οὐκ ἔχει. (John iv. 44.) 10. ἐκ τῆς φυλῆς Ἰούδα. (Rev. v. 5.)

¹ The context calls for the auxiliary *will* or *would.*

IX.

§ 16. **Verbs in -ω, in the present, optative, active.**

[βουλεύοιμι, *I might advise.*]
[βουλεύοις, *thou mightest advise.*]
πρὶν ἔχοι, *before he has.* (Acts xxv. 16.)
[βουλεύοιμεν, *we might advise.*]
εἰ πάσχοιτε, *if you suffer.* (1 Peter iii. 14.)
εἰ ἔχοιεν, *if they had.* (Acts xxiv. 19.)

Rem. a. The fundamental idea of the optative mode does not differ from that of the subjunctive ; but the conceptions of the former are *more subjective,* looking less to outward realization than those of the latter.

Rem. b. In the optative as in the subjunctive mode, *tense* distinctions have comparatively little to do with the indication of *time,* which, in dependent sentences, is determined by the leading verb.

Rem. c. This mode is rarely used by the N. T. writers.

§ 17. **Nouns of the first declension, in the plural number, with the article.**

N. αἱ ἁμαρτίαι, *the sins.* (Matt. ix. 2.)
G. τῶν ἁμαρτιῶν, *of our sins.* (Col. i. 14.)
D. ταῖς ἁμαρτίαις, *to our sins.* (1 Peter ii. 24.)
A. τὰς ἁμαρτίας, *the sins.* (Heb. ii. 17.)

N. οἱ προφῆται, *the prophets.* (Matt. vii. 12.)
G. τῶν προφητῶν, *of the prophets.* (Matt. xvi. 14.)
D. τοῖς προφήταις, *to the prophets.* (Luke vi. 23.)
A. τοὺς προφήτας, *the prophets.* (Matt. v. 17.)

Rem. The article often has the force of a possessive pronoun, whose person and number must be determined from the context.

* The T. R. reads ὁ Ἰησοῦς. It is not uncommon for proper names to take the article.

TRANSLATE

1. ἀπὸ τῆς Γαλιλαίας εἰς τὸν Ἰορδάνην πρὸς τὸν Ἰωάννην. (Matt. iii. 13.) 2. ἐγὼ χρείαν ἔχω. (Matt. iii. 14.) 3. παρὰ τὴν θάλασσαν τῆς Γαλιλαίας. (Matt. iv. 18.) 4. εἰς τὴν θάλασσαν. (Matt. iv. 18.) 5. οὕτως γὰρ ἐδίωξαν τοὺς προφήτας. (Matt. v. 12.) 6. ὃς ἂν φονεύσῃ. (Matt. v. 21.) 7. χρείαν ἔχετε. (Matt. vi. 8.) 8. ὅταν νηστεύητε. (Matt. vi. 16.) 9. ἐπὶ τῆς γῆς. (Matt. vi. 19.) 10. κλέπται διορύσσουσιν καὶ κλέπτουσιν. (Matt. vi. 19.)

X.

§ 18. Verbs in -ω, in the aorist, optative, active.

[βουλεύσαιμι, *I might advise.*]
[βουλεύσαις, *thou mightest advise.*]
περισσεύσαι, may [*he*] *cause to abound.* (1 Thess. iii. 12.)
[βουλεύσαιμεν, *we might advise.*]
[βουλεύσαιτε, *you might advise.*]
τί ἂν ποιήσειαν, or -αιεν, *what they should do.* (Luke vi. 11.)

Rem. On the aorist optative, see § 5, *Rem. a,* and § 16, *Rem. a, b.*

§ 19. Nouns of the second declension, with the article.

Singular.

N. ὁ [ἡ] ἄνθρωπος.* (Matt. xii. 35.)	τὸ ἔργον. (Rom. xi. 6.)
G. τοῦ [τῆς] ἀνθρώπου. (Matt. viii. 20.)	τοῦ ἔργου. (1 Thess. i. 3.)
D. τῷ [τῇ] ἀνθρώπῳ. (Matt. xviii. 7.)	τῷ ἔργῳ. (1 Cor. xv. 58.)
A. τὸν [τὴν] ἄνθρωπον. (Matt. xv. 11.)	τὸ ἔργον. (Mark xiii. 34.)
V. ἄνθρωπε. (Rom. ii. 1.)	

Plural.

N. -οἱ [αἱ] ἄνθρωποι. (Luke vi. 26.)	τὰ ἔργα. (John iii. 19.)
G. τῶν ἀνθρώπων. (Matt. v. 13.)	τῶν ἔργων. (Heb. iv. 3.)
D. τοῖς [ταῖς] ἀνθρώποις. (Matt. vi. 5.)	τοῖς ἔργοις. (John x. 38.)
A. τοὺς [τὰς] ἀνθρώπους. (Luke vii. 31.)	τὰ ἔργα. (Matt. v. 16.)

Rem. a. Nouns of the second declension end regularly in ος and ον, exceptionally in ως. Those in -ον are of the neuter gender ; the rest are either masculine, feminine, or common.

---

* Ἄνθρωπος is of the com. gender, though found in the N. T. with the masc. article only.

Rem. b. The oblique cases of those in -ωs all end in ω [the D. in φ], the A. having also a form in -ων. The A. ἀνώγεον (T. R. Mark xiv. 15, Luke xxii. 12) has, in classical Greek, nominatives in ων and ωs.

Rem. c. In John xix. 36, ὀστοῦν is a contraction from ὀστέον.

Rem. d. From νόος has arisen, by contraction, νοῦς (1 Cor. xiv. 14), which, however, is inflected after the analogy of the third declension, thus : G. νοός (Rom. vii. 23), D. νοΐ (Rom. xiv. 5), A. νοῦν (Luke xxiv. 45). The forms πλοός (Acts xxvii. 9) and πλοῦν (Acts xxi. 7) also point to a nominative πλοῦς = πλόος.

Rem. e. In neuters, whether of the second or third declension, the accusative is always like the nominative and in the plural ends in *a*.

XI.

TRANSLATE

1. ἐξουσίαν ἔχει ὁ υἱὸς τοῦ ἀνθρώπου[1] ἐπὶ τῆς γῆς. (Matt. ix. 6.)   2. ὁ δὲ υἱὸς τοῦ ἀνθρώπου οὐκ ἔχει ποῦ τὴν κεφαλὴν κλίνῃ. (Matt. viii. 20.)· 3. καὶ λέγουσιν · ἰδοὺ ἄνθρωπος φάγος[2] καὶ οἰνοπότης, τελωνῶν φίλος καὶ ἁμαρτωλῶν. (Matt. xi. 19.)   4. λέγει τῷ ἀνθρώπῳ. (Matt. xii. 13.)   5. οὐ γὰρ βλέπεις εἰς πρόσωπον ἀνθρώπων,[3] ἀλλ'[4] ἐπ'[4] ἀληθείας[5] τὴν ὁδὸν τοῦ θεοῦ[6] διδάσκεις. (Mark xii. 14.)   6. τὰ ἔργα τοῦ θεοῦ. (John vi. 28.)   7. τὰ μνημεῖα τῶν προφητῶν. (Luke xi. 47.)   8. ἐν ταῖς ἡμέραις τοῦ υἱοῦ τοῦ ἀνθρώπου. (Luke xvii. 26.)   9. ἡ βασιλεία τοῦ θεοῦ. (Luke xvii. 21.)   10. ἐπὶ τὸν υἱὸν τοῦ ἀνθρώπου. (John i. 52.)

[1] Nouns used in their widest comprehension, or in a generic sense, may take the article.

[2] In translating the words ἄνθρωπος φάγος, we may either insert a relative phrase, thus : *a man [who is] a glutton*, or we may drop the word *man* and say simply *a glutton*.

[3] ἀνθρώπων may be translated either *of men* or *men's* ; but if the former rendering is used, an article must be supplied with πρόσωπον.

[4] Final short vowels, except ΰ, may be *elided*, when the next word begins with a vowel. This *elision* is indicated by an apostrophe in the place of the vowel.

[5] In connection with ἀληθείας we cannot translate ἐπί literally, but we may render the two words by the equivalent adverb *truly*, or the phrase *of a truth.*

[6] To distinguish Jehovah from the heathen deities, he was called ὁ θεός, THE *god*, and sometimes ὁ θεὸς τῶν θεῶν, *the god of the gods*, or *the supreme god.* See Ps. cxxxvi. 2 (in the Septuagint cxxxv. 2).

XII.

§ 20. Verbs in -ω, in the present, imperative, active.

πίστευε, *believe (thou).* (Mark v. 36.)
βασιλευέτω, *let* [*it*] *reign.* (Rom. vi. 12.)
πιστεύετε, *believe (ye).* (Mark i. 15.)
δουλευέτωσαν, *let them serve.* (1 Tim. vi. 2.)

Rem. General precepts commonly take the form of the *present* imperative, while *particular* commands are put in the *aorist* (imperative or subjunctive), in accordance with the usual distinction between these tenses. There is no distinction in point of time between the present and the aorist imperative.

§ 21. The third declension of nouns.

Rem. a. To the third declension belong all nouns which have one more syllable in the genitive than in the nominative. They are of all genders and have a great variety of endings.

Rem. b. The true stem, in nouns of this declension, is usually to be sought in the genitive case, having undergone some euphonic change in the nominative.

§ 22. Nouns of the third declension with the genitive ending ατος.

Singular.	Plural.
N. βρῶμα. (John iv. 34.)	βρώματα. (1 Cor. vi. 13.)
G. βρώματος. (Rom. xiv. 20.)	βρωμάτων. (1 Tim. iv. 3.)
D. βρώματι. (Rom. xiv. 15.)	βρώμασι(ν.) (1 Cor. vi. 13.)
A. βρῶμα. (Rom. xiv. 15.)	βρώματα. (Matt. xiv. 15.)

Rem. a. All nouns belonging here are neuter.

Rem. b. They end either in α, αρ (only φρέαρ), ας, υ (only γόνυ), or ωρ (only ὕδωρ).

Rem. c. In Rom. xiv. 21 and 1 Cor. viii. 13, we find the acc. pl. of κρέας contracted, by syncope, to κρέα.

Rem. d. As the dat. of γῆρας, we find, in Luke i. 36, the syncopated form γήρᾳ (T. R.) or γήρει (Tisch.).

Rem. e. The linguals, τ, δ, θ, ζ, are always dropped before σ, κ, γ, χ. Hence βρώμασιν for βρώματσιν.

Rem. f. In the dative plural, the final ν is often dropped before a consonant.

TRANSLATE

1. μὴ ἕνεκεν βρώματος κατάλυε τὸ ἔργον τοῦ θεοῦ. (Rom. xiv. 20.) 2. καὶ ἤνοιξεν τὸ φρέαρ τῆς ἀβύσσου. (Rev. ix. 2.) 3. θησαυρίζετε θησαυροὺς ἐν οὐρανῷ. (Matt. vi. 20.) 4. ἐν τοῖς ὕδασιν. (Matt. viii. 32.) 5. καὶ ἰδοὺ φωνὴ ἐκ τῶν οὐρανῶν. (Matt. iii. 17.) 6. ὑπὸ τοῦ πνεύματος. (Matt. iv. 1.) 7. παραβολὴν ἐλάλησεν. (Matt. xiii. 33.) 8. σημεῖα ἐν ἡλίῳ καὶ σελήνη καὶ ἄστροις. (Luke xxi. 25.) 9. ἐν ταῖς ἡμέραις Ἡρώδου. (Luke i. 5.) 10. ἐν πνεύματι καὶ ἀληθείᾳ. (John iv. 24.)

XIII

§ 23. **Verbs in -ω, in the aorist, imperative, active.**

πίστευσον, *believe (thou).* (Acts. xvi. 31.)
ἀκουσάτω, *let him hear.* (Rev. xiii. 9.)
πιστεύσατε, *believe (ye).* (John x. 38.) *
γαμεσάτωσαν, *let them marry.* (1 Cor. vii. 9.)

Rem. See § 20, *Rem.*

§ 24. **Nouns of the third declension with the genitive endings δος and θος.**

Singular.	Plural.
N. ἐλπίς. (Acts xvi. 19.)	πόδες. (Acts v. 9.)
G. ἐλπίδος. (Acts xxiii. 6.)	ποδῶν. (Matt. v. 35.)
D. ἐλπίδι. (Acts ii. 26.)	ποσί(ν). (Matt. vii. 6.)
A. ἐλπίδα. (Acts xxiv. 15.)	πόδας. (Matt. xv. 30.

Rem. a. The nouns belonging here are those in -αις G. -αιδος (only ὁ ἡ παῖς), -ας G. -αδος, -εις G. -ειδος, -ις G. -ιδος, -ους G. -οδος (only ὁ πούς), -υς G. -υδος, and -ις G. -ιθος (only ὁ ἡ ὄρνις). They are all feminine excepting παῖς, πούς, and ὄρνις.

Rem b. In Rev. xx. 1, some MSS. have κλεῖν, instead of κλεῖδα, as the acc. sing. of κλείς. In one or two instances we find the acc. pl. κλεῖδας syncopated into κλεῖς.

---

* Tisch. reads πιστεύετε.

Rem. c. In the N. T., the acc. sing. of ἔρις is only ἔριν (Phil. i. 15). Besides the regular nom. pl. ἔριδες, the syncopated form ἔρεις occurs in some texts, and the same form is used for the acc. pl. in Titus iii. 9.

§ 25. Nouns of the third declension with the genitive endings ητος, ιτος, and ωτος.

Rem. a. The corresponding nom. endings are ης, ι or ις, and ως.

Rem. b. Of the nouns belonging here, φῶς and μέλι are neuter and inflected like βρῶμα (§ 22) : the rest are masculine (excepting χάρις, ἐσθής and abstracts in -οτης and -υτης), and are inflected like the examples in § 24.

Rem. c. We may also place here the neuter noun οὖς (G. ὠτός), which in the Doric dialect had the form ὦς.

Rem. d. The acc. sing. of χάρις is much oftener χάριν than χάριτα.

TRANSLATE

1. ἀκούσατε τὴν παραβολήν. (Matt. xiii. 18.) 2. ἀκουσάτωσαν. (Luke xvi. 29.) 3. περὶ Ἡρωδιάδος. (Luke iii. 19.) 4. ὁ θεὸς τῆς ἐλπίδος. (Rom. xv. 13.) 5. πόδας ἔνιψεν. (1 Tim. v. 10.) 6. ἡ κλεὶς τοῦ φρέατος τῆς ἀβύσσου. (Rev. ix. 1.) 7. ἔχω τὰς κλεῖς. (Rev. i. 18.) 8. μανθανέτωσαν. (Titus iii. 14.) 9. ἀδελφέ. (Phil. 20.) 10. εἰς τὴν Ἑλλάδα. (Acts xx. 2.)

XIV.

§ 26. Verbs in -ω, in the infinitive, active.

Present. πιστεύειν, to believe. (1 Tim. i. 16.)
Aorist. πιστεῦσαι, to believe. (John v. 44.)
Perfect. πεποιηκέναι, to have done. (John xii. 18.)

Rem. a. The *modal* distinction noticed in § 1, *Rem. a*, and § 5, *Rem. a*, between the present and aorist tenses, must be borne in mind with regard to the infinitive forms. In these tenses, the distinction of *time*, which is found in the indicative mode, ordinarily disappears in the infinitive.

Rem. b. When the time element is retained, the present infinitive may often be translated by the present indicative, and the aorist by the imperfect or pluperfect indicative preceded by *that*.

Rem. c. The perfect is equivalent sometimes to the perfect and sometimes to the pluperfect indicative preceded by *that.* Thus, in John xii.
18, the Greek idiom, *heard him to have done,* becomes, in good English,
heard that he had done.

§ 27. Nouns of the third declension with the genitive end-ings κος, γος, χος, κτος, πος, βος.

Rem. a. The first four endings belong to nouns in -ξ, the last two
to nouns in -ψ.

Rem. b. Two anomalous nouns may be placed here, γυνή (G. γυναικός
V. γύναι) and γάλα (G. γάλακτος).

Rem. c. These nouns are all either masculine or feminine (with the
exception of τὸ γάλα), and are inflected like the examples in § 24.

Rem. d. In ἀλώπηξ (G. ἀλώπεκος), ε is lengthened to η only in the
nominative singular.

TRANSLATE

1. τύπτειν τοὺς παῖδας καὶ τὰς παιδίσκας. (Luke xii. 45.)   2. νίπτειν
τοὺς πόδας τῶν μαθητῶν. (John xiii. 5.)   3. τίς ποιμαίνει ποίμνην καὶ
ἐκ τοῦ γάλακτος τῆς ποίμνης οὐκ ἐσθίει; (1 Cor. ix. 7.)   4. χωρὶς γυναι-
κῶν καὶ παιδίων. (Matt. xiv. 21.)   5. πρὸς γυναῖκα χήραν. (Luke iv.
26.)   6. μνημονεύετε¹ τῆς γυναικὸς Λώτ.² (Luke xvii. 32.)   7. τῇ γυναικὶ
ἔλεγον.³ (John iv. 42.)   8. γύναι, τί κλαίεις; (John xx. 13.)   9. γυνὴ
ὀνόματι⁴ Λυδία. (Acts. xvi. 14.)   10. ἐδίωξεν τὴν γυναῖκα. (Rev. xii. 13.)

¹ See § 82, VI.   ³ Plural number.
² See § 43.   ⁴ "by name." See § 82, XVI.

XV.

§ 28. Active participles of verbs in -ω, in the nominative, singular, masculine.

Present. πιστεύων, *believing.* (Acts xxiv. 14.)
Future. κακώσων, *about to harm.* (1 Peter iii. 13.)
Aorist. πιστεύσας, *having believed.* (Mark xvi. 16.)*
Perfect. πεπιστευκώς, *having believed.* (Acts xvi. 34.)

---

* Mark xvi. 9-20 is not considered genuine by Tischendorf.

Rem. a. Participles have masc., fem. and neut. endings, and are inflected like nouns and adjectives. See § 61.

Rem. b. Although the aorist and perfect participles sometimes require the same translation, yet they are not identical in force, since the former describes an action as having occurred previously to, the latter as already completed at, the time of some other event.

§ 29. Nouns of the third declension with the genitive ending ντος.

Singular.	Plural.
N. ἄρχων. (Matt. ix. 18.)	ἄρχοντες. (Matt. xx. 25.)
G. ἄρχοντος. (Matt. ix. 23.)	ἀρχόντων. (Luke xiv. 1.)
D. ἄρχοντι. (Matt. ix. 34.)	ἄρχουσι(ν). (Acts xiv. 5.)
A. ἄρχοντα. (Matt. xii. 58.)	ἄρχοντας. (Luke xxiii. 13.)

Rem. a. The nouns belonging here are those in -ας G. -αντος, -ης G. -εντος (only three proper names derived from the Latin), -ους G. -οντος (only ὀδούς), and -ων G. -οντος, all which are masculine.*

Rem. b. ν is often dropped before σ, and if a following lingual has also been dropped (see § 22, *Rem. e*) the preceding vowel is generally lengthened. Thus we find ἄρχουσιν and not ἄρχοντσιν.

TRANSLATE

1. ἐλπίδα ἔχων. (Acts. xxiv. 15.) 2. εἰς τὴν οἰκίαν τοῦ ἄρχοντος. (Matt. ix. 23.) 3. ὀφθαλμὸν ἀντὶ ὀφθαλμοῦ καὶ ὀδόντα ἀντὶ ὀδόντος. (Matt. v. 38.) 4. ὁ κλαυθμὸς καὶ ὁ βρυγμὸς τῶν ὀδόντων (Matt. viii. 12.) 5. ἔβρυχον τοὺς ὀδόντας. (Acts vii. 54.) 6. ἔμπροσθεν τῶν ποδῶν τοῦ ἀγγέλου. (Rev. xxii. 8.) 7. ἀκουέτω. (Matt. xiii. 9.) 8. οὐ τί ἐγὼ θέλω ἀλλὰ τί σύ. (Mark. xiv. 36.) 9. μὴ οὖν βασιλευέτω ἡ ἁμαρτία. (Rom. vi. 12.) 10. λῦσαι τὸν ἱμάντα. (Mark. i. 7.)

XVI.

§ 30. Verbs in -ω, in the present, indicative, passive (and middle).

τί διώκομαι; *why am I persecuted?* (Gal. v. 11.)
σὺ ἐπονομάζῃ, *thou art named,* or *called.* (Rom. ii. 17.)

---

* As the G. of Σολομών, the T. R. has Σολομῶντος, but Tisch. usually Σολομῶνος.

πιστεύεται, *it is believed*, or, *man believes*. (Rom. x. 10.)
ἡμεῖς ἀνακρινόμεθα, *we are examined*. (Acts iv. 9.)
ἄγεσθε, *you are led*. (Gal. v. 18.)
ἄγονται, [*they*] *are led*. (Rom. viii. 14.)

Rem. a. The *middle* voice does not differ, in its forms, from the *passive*, except in the future and aorist tenses. In force, it is either reflexive, or denotes that the agent does something or causes something to be done for himself. Sometimes it seems to be simply equivalent to the active voice. For examples, see §§ 36 and 41.

Rem. b. If, in combining prepositions and verbs, two vowels come together, the preposition (unless it be περί or πρό) loses its final vowel. Thus we find ἐπονομάζῃ and not ἐπιονομάζῃ.

Rem. c. In the second pers. sing. the termination ει is sometimes found.

§ 31. Nouns of the third declension with the genitive ending ἐως.

Singular.	Plural.
N. βασιλεύς. (Matt. xiv. 9.)	βασιλεῖς. (Matt. xvii. 25.)
G. βασιλέως. (Matt. ii. 1.)	βασιλέων. (Matt. xi. 8.)
D. βασιλεῖ. (Matt. xviii. 23.)	βασιλεῦσι(ν). (Rev. x. 11.)
A. βασιλέα. (Matt. i. 6.)	βασιλεῖς. (Luke xxi. 12.)
V. βασιλεῦ. (Acts xxv. 26.)	

Rem. a. Nouns with the genitive ending εως have as nominative endings αυς (only ναύς), ευς, ης (only Μωσῆς), ι (only σίναπι), ις, υς (only πῆχυς).

Rem. b. Those in -ευς and -ης are masculine, those in -ι neuter, and the rest (almost without exception) feminine.

Rem. c. Those in -αυς, -ις and -υς form the accusative in ν. Thus from ναύς we have the accusative ναῦν (Acts xxvii. 41), from πίστις the A. πίστιν (Matt. xvii. 20), from πῆχυς the A. πῆχυν (Matt. vi. 27).

Rem. d. Μωσῆς (in most modern editions Μωυσῆς) has a D. in -ῇ and an A. in -ῆν, besides the regular forms.

Rem. e. In the printed editions, πήχεων is contracted to πηχῶν; but some of the MSS. have the uncontracted form.

TRANSLATE

1. λεπροὶ καθαρίζονται. (Matt. xi. 5.) 2. ἐν τοῖς οἴκοις τῶν βασιλέων. (Matt. xi. 8.) 3. πιστεύεις, βασιλεῦ Ἀγρίππα, τοῖς προφήταις; (Acts xxvi. 27.) 4. καὶ ἤκουσεν ὁ βασιλεὺς Ἡρώδης. (Mark vi. 14.)

5. ἐν ταῖς ἡμέραις Ἡρώδου τοῦ βασιλέως τῆς Ἰουδαίας. (Luke i. 5.)
6. ὁ ἄρχων τῶν βασιλέων τῆς γῆς. (Rev. i. 5.) 7. ἐκ τοῦ στόματος τοῦ
ψευδοπροφήτου. (Rev. xvi. 13.) 8. ἐγὼ βρῶσιν ἔχω. (John iv. 32.)
9. ἐὰν ἔχητε πίστιν ὡς κόκκον σινάπεως. (Matt. xvii. 20.) 10. διαστρέ-
ψαι τὸν ἀνθύπατον ἀπὸ τῆς πίστεως. (Acts. xiii. 8.)

XVII.

§ 32. Verbs in -ω, in the imperfect, indicative, passive
(and middle).

> ἐνεκοπτόμην, *I was hindered.* (Rom. xv. 22.)
> ἤρχου, *thou wast coming.* (Acts ix. 17.)
> ἤγετο, *he was led.* (Luke iv. 1.)
> κατειχόμεθα, *we were held, or bound.* (Rom. vii. 6.)
> ἤγεσθε, *you were led.* (1 Cor. xii. 2.)
> ἤγοντο, [*they*] *were led.* (Luke xxiii. 32.)

Rem. a. Whenever ν comes before a palatal, it is changed into γ.
Thus in Acts xxiv. 4 we find ἐγκόπτω instead of ἐνκόπτω. The introduction of a vowel after the γ changes the consonant back to ν, as in
ἐνεκοπτόμην.

§ 33. Nouns of the third declension with the genitive
ending ρος preceded by a vowel.

Singular.	Plural.
N. χείρ. (Luke i. 66.)	χεῖρες. (Acts xx. 34.)
G. χειρός. (Luke i. 71.)	χειρῶν. (Luke iv. 11.)
D. χειρί. (Luke iii. 17.)	χερσί(ν). (Luke vi. 1.)
A. χεῖρα. (Luke v. 13.)	χεῖρας. (Luke iv. 40.)

Rem. a. The nouns belonging here are those in -αρ G. -αρος, -ειρ G.
-ειρος (only χείρ), -ηρ G. -ηρος, -ηρ G. -ερος, -υρ G. -υρος (only πῦρ), -υς
G. -υρος (only μάρτυς), and -ωρ G. -ορος.

Rem. b. These nouns are all masculine, except ἡ χείρ and τὸ πῦρ.

Rem. c. The D. pl. of μάρτυς is μάρτυσιν. (Acts x. 41.)

TRANSLATE

1. ἐθεραπεύοντο. (Acts xxviii. 9.) 2. βάλλει ὕδωρ εἰς τὸν νιπτῆρα.
(John xiii. 5.) 3. διὰ τῆς ἐπιθέσεως τῶν χειρῶν τῶν ἀποστόλων. (Acts

viii. 18.)   4. διὰ χειρὸς Βαρνάβα καὶ Σαύλου. (Acts xi. 30.)   5. Παῦλος κατέσεισεν τῇ χειρὶ¹ τῷ λαῷ. (Acts xxi. 40.)   6. κατασείσας τὴν χεῖρα. (Acts xix. 33.)   7. πολλάκις γὰρ πίπτει εἰς τὸ πῦρ καὶ πολλάκις εἰς τὸ ὕδωρ. (Matt. xvii. 15.)   8. γλῶσσαι ὡσεὶ πυρός. (Acts ii. 3.)   9. εἰς τὴν λίμνην τοῦ πυρός. (Rev. xx. 10.)   10. κατὰ τὸν ἄρχοντα τῆς ἐξουσίας τοῦ ἀέρος. (Eph. ii. 2.)

¹ See § 82, XIV.

XVIII.

§ 34. Verbs in -ω, in the future, indicative, passive.

σωθήσομαι,* I shall be cured. (Matt. ix. 21.)
σωθήσῃ, thou shalt be saved. (Acts xi. 14.)
σωθήσεται, he will be kept safe. (John x. 9.)
σωθησόμεθα, we shall be saved. (Rom. v. 9.)
ἀχθήσεσθε, you will be led. (Matt. x. 18.)
βασανισθήσονται, they will be tormented. (Rev. xx. 10.)

Rem. a. When two mutes come together, they must both be either smooth, middle, or rough, and the character of the second determines that of the first. Thus, in ἀχθήσεσθε, the rough tense-characteristic θ necessitates the change of the middle mute γ into its corresponding rough. See p. 3, 4, Rem. c.

Rem. b. When τ, δ, θ, or ς comes before τ, δ, θ, ς, or μ, the former consonant is usually changed into σ. Thus instead of βασανιζθήσονται we have βασανισθήσονται.

§ 35. Nouns of the third declension with the genitive ending ρος preceded by a consonant.

	Singular.	Plural.
N.	πατήρ. (Matt. v. 48.)	πατέρες. (Luke vi. 23.)
G.	πατρός. (Matt. ii. 22.)	πατέρων. (Luke i. 17.)
D.	πατρί. (Matt. vi. 1.)	πατράσι(ν). (Acts. vii. 44.)
A.	πατέρα. (Matt. iv. 22.)	πατέρας. (Acts. vii. 19.)
V.	πάτερ. (Matt. vi. 9.)	

* The pres. act. of this verb is σώζω, but the fut. and aor. pass. are derived from a form without the ς.

Rem. a. Five nouns (ἡ μήτηρ, ἡ θυγάτηρ, ἡ γαστήρ, ὁ πατήρ, ὁ ἀνήρ), which would regularly have the ending εροs in the G., drop the ε in the G. and D. sing. and D. pl. In the D. pl. they also insert α before the case ending.

Rem. b. In ἀνήρ, δ always takes the place of ε.

TRANSLATE

1. ἐπιστρέψαι καρδίας πατέρων ἐπὶ τέκνα. (Luke i. 17.) 2. ἐκάκωσεν τοὺς πατέρας. (Acts vii. 19.) 3. πατέρα ἔχομεν τὸν Ἀβραάμ. (Matt. iii. 9.) 4. πάτερ, κύριε τοῦ οὐρανοῦ καὶ τῆς γῆς. (Matt. xi. 25.) 5. ἡ μήτηρ τῶν υἱῶν Ζεβεδαίου. (Matt. xx. 20.) 6. μετὰ τῶν ἀνδρῶν. (Luke xi. 31.) 7. ἀνὴρ ὀνόματι[1] Ἰωσήφ. (Luke xxiii. 50.) 8. ἄνδρα οὐκ ἔχω. (John iv. 17.) 9. ἐκ τῶν θυγατέρων Ἀαρών. (Luke i. 5.) 10. ὁ πατὴρ τοῦ παιδίου ἔλεγεν · πιστεύω. (Mark ix. 24.)

[1] See § 82, XVI.

XIX.

§ 36. Verbs in -ω, in the future, indicative, middle.

ἐγὼ καυχήσομαι, *I will boast.* (2 Cor. xi. 18.)
ἀκούσῃ, *thou shalt hear.* (Acts xxv. 22.)
ζήσεται, *[he] shall,* or *will, live.* (John xi. 25.)
ἀκουσόμεθα, *we will hear.* (Acts xvii. 32.)
ἀκούσεσθε, *you shall hear.* (Acts iii. 22.)
ἀκούσονται, *they will hear.* (Acts xxi. 22.)

Rem. a. Those verbs which are not used in the active voice, but which, in their passive or middle forms, have an active signification, are called passive or middle *deponents.* Some verbs are deponent only in particular tenses.

Rem. b. In some MSS. and editions, ει is also found as an ending of the second pers. sing. in the fut. indic. middle.

§ 37. Nouns of the third declension with the genitive ending νος.

Rem. a. These nouns are inflected like χείρ (§ 33), but drop ν before -σιν in the D. plural, the preceding vowel remaining the same as in the genitive.

Rem. b. They have the endings ην G. ηνος, ην G. ενος, υ G. υνος (only ὠδίν), ις G. ινος (only Σαλαμίς), ων G. ωνος, ων G. ονος.

Rem. c. φρήν, ὠδίν, Σαλαμίς, and ἅλων are fem., the rest masc.

TRANSLATE

1. ὥσπερ ὁ ποιμὴν ἀφορίζει τὰ πρόβατα ἀπὸ τῶν ἐρίφων. (Matt. xxv. 32.) 2. ἤκουσα φωνὴν ἐκ τοῦ οὐρανοῦ. (Rev. x. 4.) 3. ὑπάγετε καὶ ὑμεῖς εἰς τὸν ἀμπελῶνα. (Matt. xx. 4.) 4. τί ποιήσει ὁ κύριος τοῦ ἀμπελῶνος; (Mark xii. 9.) 5. μὴ οὐκ ἔχομεν ἐξουσίαν ἀδελφὴν γυναῖκα περιάγειν; (1 Cor. ix. 5.) 6. τίς φυτεύει ἀμπελῶνα; (1 Cor. ix. 7.) 7. μὴ ἀδικήσητε τὴν γῆν μήτε τὴν θάλασσαν μήτε τὰ δένδρα. (Rev. vii. 3.) 8. ἰδοὺ ἔρχεται μετὰ τῶν νεφελῶν. (Rev. i. 7.) 9. καὶ ἐβλασφήμησαν οἱ ἄνθρωποι τὸν θεὸν ἐκ τῆς πληγῆς τῆς χαλάζης. (Rev. xvi. 21.) 10. βασιλεὺς βασιλέων καὶ κύριος κυρίων. (Rev. xix. 16.)

XX.

§ 38. **Verbs in -ω, in the aorist, indicative, passive.**

ἐπιστεύθην ἐγώ, *I was intrusted with.* (1 Tim. i. 11.)
σὺ ἐγεννήθης, *thou wast born.* (John ix. 34.)
ἐπιστεύθη, [*it*] *was believed.* (2 Thess. i. 10.)
ἐσώθημεν, *we were saved.* (Rom. viii. 24.)
ἠγοράσθητε, *you were bought.* (1 Cor. vi. 20.)
ἐπιστεύθησαν, *they were intrusted with.* (Rom. iii. 2.)

Rem. Many verbs insert σ before θ in the aor. pass.

§ 39. **Nouns of the third declension with the genitive ending ους.**

Singular.	Plural.
N. ὄρος. (Luke iii. 5.)	ὄρη. (Rev. xvi. 20.)
G. ὄρους. (Matt. v. 14.)	ὀρέων. (Rev. vi. 15.)
D. ὄρει. (Matt. xvii. 20.)	ὄρεσι(ν). (Mark. v. 5.)
A. ὄρος. (Matt. iv. 8.)	ὄρη. (Matt. xviii. 12.)

Rem. a. There belong here all neuters in -ος, the masculines Διοτρεφής and Ἑρμογένης (which, however, occur in the N. T. only in the nominative) and the feminines αἰδώς (found only in the genitive) and πειθώ (D. πειθοῖ, found as a various reading in 1 Cor. ii. 4). See § 47, *Rem. b.*

Rem. b. In the neuters, the ending ους has been contracted from εος, ει from εϊ, and η from εα. The G. pl. -εων is usually contracted to -ων, ὁρέων (Rev. vi. 15) and χειλέων (Heb. xiii. 15) being exceptions. The G. αἰδοῦς (1 Tim. ii. 9) = αἰδόος.

§ 40. Nouns of the third declension with the genitive ending οος. Cf. § 19, *Rem. d.*

Rem. Only ὁ ἡ βοῦς and ὁ χοῦς belong here. In the A. sing. they have βοῦν (Luke xiii. 15) and χοῦν (Mark vi. 11), the latter word being found in no other case. In the pl., the G. βοῶν (Luke xvi. 19) and the A. βόας (John ii. 14) occur.

TRANSLATE

1. ἀνήχθημεν. (Acts xxvii. 2.) 2. ἐβαρήθημεν. (2 Cor. i. 8.) 3. ἀναβαίνει εἰς τὸ ὄρος. (Mark iii. 13.) 4. ἐν τοῖς ὄρεσιν. (Mark v. 5.) 5. τότε ἄρξονται λέγειν τοῖς ὄρεσιν. (Luke xxiii. 30.) 6. ἡ φιλαδελφία μενέτω. (Heb. xiii. 1.) 7. διὰ τὸ μὴ ἔχειν[1] βάθος γῆς. (Matt. xiii. 5.) 8. ἐμβλέψατε εἰς τὰ πετεινὰ τοῦ οὐρανοῦ. (Matt. vi. 26.) 9. ἐπὶ ἡγεμόνας δὲ καὶ βασιλεῖς ἀχθήσεσθε. (Matt. x. 18.) 10. ὑμεῖς οὖν ἀκούσατε τὴν παραβολήν. (Matt. xiii. 18.)

[1] The inf. with the neut. article is equivalent to a participial substantive.

XXI.

§ 41. Verbs in -ω, in the aorist, indicative, middle.

ἐνιψάμην, *I washed.* (John ix. 15.)
κατηρτίσω, *thou didst prepare.* (Matt. xxi. 16.)
ἐνίψατο, *he washed.* (John ix. 7.)
ἡμεῖς ἐδεξάμεθα, *we received.* (Acts xxviii. 21.)
ἠτήσασθε, *you asked.* (Acts iii. 14.)
ἠτήσαντο, *they asked.* (Acts xiii. 28.)

§ 42. Nouns of the third declension with the genitive ending υος.

Rem. a. These end, in the N., in υ and υς, and are inflected similarly to the examples in § 24, except that they have the termination ν in the accusative, instead of a. Cf. § 31, *Rem. c.*

Rem. b. Those in *-υ* are neuter, those in *-υς* feminine, with the following exceptions : ὁ βότρυς, ὁ ἰχθύς, ὁ στάχυς, and ὁ ἡ ὗς.

§43. Nouns borrowed from the Hebrew.

Rem. Many of these are indeclinable in their Greek form, some are inflected like the examples already given, and others have a peculiar declension. 'Ιησοῦς has G. D. and V. 'Ιησοῦ and A. 'Ιησοῦν. Λευείς (or Λευΐς) has G. Λευεί (or Λευΐ) A. Λευείν (or Λευΐν).

TRANSLATE

1. ἀπήγξατο. (Matt. xxvii. 5.)   2. ᾐτήσατο τὸ σῶμα τοῦ 'Ιησοῦ. (Matt. xxvii. 58.)   3. ἀπενίψατο τὰς χεῖρας ἀπέναντι τοῦ ὄχλου. (Matt. xxvii. 24.)   4. ᾐτήσαντο βασιλέα. (Acts xiii. 21.)   5. τρύγησον τοὺς βότρυας. (Rev. xiv. 18.)   6. ἀπὸ τοῦ πλήθους τῶν ἰχθύων. (John xxi. 6.)   7. ἤρξαντο τίλλειν στάχυας καὶ ἐσθίειν. (Matt. xii. 1.)   8. ἔρχονται πρὸς τὸν 'Ιησοῦν. (Mark v. 15.)   9. ὁ Πέτρος λέγει τῷ 'Ιησοῦ. (Mark ix. 5.)   10. ἕξεις θησαυρὸν ἐν οὐρανῷ. (Mark x. 21.)

XXII.

§44. Verbs in -ω, in the perfect, indicative, passive (and middle).

πεπίστευμαι, *I have been intrusted with.* (1 Cor. ix. 17.)
ἀπολέλυσαι, *thou hast been,* or *art, freed from.* (Luke xiii. 12.)
σέσωσται, *he has been cured.* (Acts iv. 9.)
ἡμεῖς γεγεννήμεθα, *we have been,* or *were, born.* (John viii. 41.)
ὑμεῖς γεγένησθε,* *you have become.* (Acts vii. 52. T. R.)
κεκράτηνται, *they are retained.* (John xx. 23.)

Rem. a. If the root ends in a consonant, the third person plural is formed by combining the nominative plural of the perfect passive participle and the verb εἰσί, the third person plural of εἰμί, *to be.*

Rem. b. Those verbs which insert σ before θ in the aor. pass. (see § 38) insert the same letter in the perf. pass. before such terminations as begin with μ or τ.   On the reduplication in this tense see § 7.

Rem. c. The perfect tense, since it represents the *result* of a com-

---

* From the irregular verb γίνομαι.

pleted action as *continuing in the present*, must often be rendered into English by the present tense.   In rare cases it is best translated by the imperfect.

§45. The inflection of adjectives, particularly those in -os, -η or -α, -ον and those in -os, -ον.

Rem. a. A large number of adjectives have three forms, one for each gender.   The feminine is always inflected like feminine nouns of the first declension (§§ 8, 10, 12, 14, 17) : the masculine and neuter may be either of the second or third declension.

Rem. b. Adjectives of three terminations with the masculine in -os have the feminine in -a, if the root ends in a vowel other than o or in ρ.

Rem. c. Many adjectives make the masculine form do service for both the masculine and feminine genders.   Some of these have also a neuter form, others not.

Rem. d. In the case of those adjectives with three forms which have the endings os (masc.), η or a (fem.), ον (neut.), the masculine and neuter are inflected like ἄνθρωπος and ἔργον (§ 19).   In the same manner are inflected those adjectives which have only the two endings os (masc. and fem.) and ον (neut.).

Rem. e. A few adjectives have the terminations ous, η, ουν, which have arisen by contraction from regular forms.   Cf. § 19, *Rem. c, d.*

Rem. f. ἵλεως (found only in Matt. xvi. 22 and Heb. viii. 12) is an Attic nominative for ἵλαος.

TRANSLATE

1. ἑτοιμάσατε τὴν ὁδὸν κυρίου. (Luke iii. 4.)   2. καὶ ὑπέστρεψεν ὁ Ἰησοῦς ἐν τῇ δυνάμει τοῦ πνεύματος εἰς τὴν Γαλιλαίαν. (Luke iv. 14.) 3. οἱ γραμματεῖς καὶ οἱ Φαρισαῖοι. (Luke v. 21.)   4. λέλυσαι ἀπὸ γυναικός; (1 Cor. vii. 27.)   5. ἡγίασται γὰρ ὁ ἀνὴρ ὁ ἄπιστος ἐν τῇ γυναικί, καὶ ἡγίασται ἡ γυνὴ ἡ ἄπιστος ἐν τῷ ἀδελφῷ.* (1 Cor. vii. 14.)   6. πεπίστευμαι τὸ εὐαγγέλιον. (Gal. ii. 7.)   7. δεδοκιμάσμεθα ὑπὸ τοῦ θεοῦ. (1 Thess. ii. 4.)   8. καὶ ὠργίσθη ὁ δράκων ἐπὶ τῇ γυναικί. (Rev. xii. 17.) 9. ἐδίωξεν τὴν γυναῖκα. (Rev. xii. 13.)   10. τίς¹ ὅμοιος τῷ θηρίῳ; (Rev. xiii. 4.)

¹ Supply in translation the verb " is."

* The T. R. has ἀνδρι.

XXIII.

§ 46. Verbs in -ω, in the pluperfect, indicative, passive (and middle).

[ἐβεβουλεύμην, *I had deliberated.*]
[ἐβεβούλευσο, *thou hadst deliberated.*]
τεθεμελίωτο, *it had been founded.* (Matt. vii. 25.) *
[ἐβεβουλεύμεθα, *we had deliberated.*]
[ἐβεβούλευσθε, *you had deliberated.*]
[ἐβεβούλευντο, *they had deliberated.*]

Rem. a. If the root ends in a consonant, the third person plural is formed by combining the nominative plural of the perfect passive participle with the verb ἦσαν, the imperfect of εἰμί, *to be.*

Rem. b. As the perfect must often be translated by the present, so the pluperfect sometimes has the force of the English imperfect.

§ 47. Adjectives in -ης, -ες.

Rem. a. Next in number to the adjectives in -ος, -η or -α, -ον, and -ος, -ον, are those in -ης (masc. and fem.), -ες (neut.). About sixty of these are found in the New Testament.

Rem. b. Adjectives with these endings are inflected like nouns of the third declension with the G. ending ους (§ 39), the masculine and feminine having the A. sing. in -η, the pl. N. in -εις, G. -ων, D. -εσι, A. -εις.

§ 48. Adjectives in -ων, -ον.

Rem. a. There are several adjectives with these endings, the majority of them anomalous comparatives (§ 57, *Rem. e, f*).

Rem. b. They are inflected like nouns of the third declension with the G. ending νος (§ 37, *Rem. a, b*), except in so far as the neuter is subject to the rule in § 19, *Rem. e.*

Rem. c. The comparatives often contract -ονα into -ω, and -ονες and -ονας into -ους.

TRANSLATE

1. ὁ θεὸς ὁ ποιήσας [1] τὸν κόσμον. (Acts xvii. 24.) 2 διελέγετο δὲ ἐν τῇ συναγωγῇ. (Acts xviii. 4.) 3. Κρίσπος δὲ ὁ ἀρχισυνάγωγος ἐπισ-

---

* See § 7, *Rem. b,* and § 9, *Rem. b.*

τευσεν τῷ κυρίῳ. (Acts xviii. 8.) 4. ἄφρονες, οὐχ ὁ ποιήσας τὸ ἔξωθεν[2] καὶ τὸ ἔσωθεν[2] ἐποίησεν; (Luke xi. 40.) 5. ἡδέως γὰρ ἀνέχεσθε τῶν ἀφρόνων. (2 Cor. xi. 19.) 6. σὺ τετήρηκας τὸν καλὸν οἶνον ἕως ἄρτι. (John ii. 10.) 7. ὁ μείζων δουλεύσει τῷ ἐλάσσονι. (Rom. ix. 12.) 8. οὐκ εἰς τὸ κρεῖσσον ἀλλὰ εἰς τὸ ἧσσον συνέρχεσθε. (1 Cor. xi. 17.) 9. με- τενόησαν εἰς τὸ κήρυγμα Ἰωνᾶ, καὶ ἰδοὺ πλεῖον Ἰωνᾶ[3] ὧδε. (Matt. xii. 41.) 10. ἐγὼ δὲ ἔχω τὴν μαρτυρίαν μείζω τοῦ Ἰωάννου.[4] (John v. 36.)

[1] A participle preceded by an article is generally best rendered by the indicative mode with a relative pronoun for its subject.
[2] An adverb preceded by an article has the force of a substantive.
[3] See § 82, XIII.
[4] 'than John,' i. e. ' than that of John.'

XXIV.

§49. Verbs in -ω, in the present, subjunctive, passive and middle.

ἐὰν προσεύχωμαι, if I pray. (1 Cor. xiv. 14.)
ὅταν προσεύχῃ, whenever thou prayest. (Matt. vi. 6.)
ἵνα δοξάζηται, that [he] may be glorified. (1 Pet. iv. 11.)
φερώμεθα, let us press on. (Heb. vi. 1.)
ὅταν προσεύχησθε, whenever you pray. (Luke xi. 2.)
ἵνα γίνωνται, that [they] may be made. (1 Cor. xvi. 2.)

§ 50. Adjectives in -υς, -εια, -υ.

Rem. These adjectives, which are few in number, have their G. masc. and neut. in -εος, sometimes contracted into -ους; otherwise they are inflected in these genders like nouns of the third declension in -υς, G. -εως (§ 31 and Rem. c). § 19, Rem. e, is to be borne in mind with regard to the N. and A. neut., the plural ending of which is -εα, sometimes contracted into -η.

§ 51. The adjective πᾶς.

Rem. The nominative forms are πᾶς, πᾶσα, πᾶν. πᾶς and πᾶν are inflected like nouns of the third declension with the G. in -αντος (§ 29), except in so far as πᾶν is subject to the rule in § 19, Rem. e, which assimilates it in declension to βρῶμα (§ 22).

TRANSLATE

1. ἄγγελος δὲ κυρίου ἐλάλησεν πρὸς Φίλιππον. (Acts viii. 26.) 2. ἐλπίδα ἔχων εἰς τὸν θεόν. (Acts xxiv. 15.) 3. οὐκ ἐπ᾽ ἄρτῳ μόνῳ ζήσεται ὁ * ἄνθρωπος. (Matt. iv. 4.) 4. ἀνεχώρησεν εἰς τὴν Γαλιλαίαν. (Matt. iv. 12.) 5. κηρύσσων τὸ εὐαγγέλιον τῆς βασιλείας καὶ θεραπεύων πᾶσαν νόσον καὶ πᾶσαν μαλακίαν ἐν τῷ λαῷ. (Matt. iv. 23.) 6. λάμπει πᾶσιν τοῖς¹ ἐν τῇ οἰκίᾳ. (Matt. v. 15.) 7. ταχὺς εἰς τὸ ἀκοῦσαι, βραδὺς εἰς τὸ λαλῆσαι, βραδὺς εἰς ὀργήν. (James i. 19.) 8. ὀργὴ γὰρ ἀνδρὸς δικαιοσύνην θεοῦ οὐ κατεργάζεται. (James i. 20.) 9. καὶ ἰδοὺ ὥρμησεν πᾶσα ἡ ἀγέλη τῶν χοίρων κατὰ τοῦ κρημνοῦ εἰς τὴν θάλασσαν. (Matt. viii. 32.) 10. καὶ περιῆγεν ὁ Ἰησοῦς τὰς πόλεις πάσας καὶ τὰς κώμας. (Matt. ix. 35.)

¹ The article when standing without a substantive is equivalent to a demonstrative pronoun.

XXV.

§ 52. Verbs in -ω, in the aorist, subjunctive, passive.

ἵνα σωθῶ, that I may be saved. (Acts xvi. 30.)
ὅπως ἂν δικαιωθῇς, that thou mayst be justified. (Rom. iii. 4.)
ἵνα σωθῇ, that she may be saved. (Mark v. 23.)
ἵνα δικαιωθῶμεν, that we might be justified. (Gal. ii. 16.)
ἵνα ὑμεῖς σωθῆτε, that you may be saved. (John v. 34.)
ἵνα σωθῶσιν, that they may be saved. (Luke viii. 12.)

§ 53. The adjectives μέγας and πολύς.

Singular.

	Masc.	Fem.	Neut.
N.	μέγας	μεγάλη	μέγα
G.	μεγάλου	μεγάλης	[μεγάλου]
D.	μεγάλῳ	μεγάλῃ	[μεγάλῳ]
A.	μέγαν	μεγάλην	μέγα
N.	πολύς	πολλή	πολύ
G.	πολλοῦ	πολλῆς	πολλοῦ
D.	πολλῷ	πολλῇ	πολλῷ
A.	πολύν	πολλήν	πολύ

* The T. R. omits ὁ.

Rem. In the plural these adjectives are inflected like those in -os of three terminations, thus : μεγάλοι, -αι, -α, *etc.* ; πολλοί, -αί, -ά, *etc.*

TRANSLATE

1. ἀλλ' οὐ πάντες ὑπήκουσαν τῷ εὐαγγελίῳ. (Rom. x. 16.)   2. ἵνα τὸ πνεῦμα σωθῇ ἐν τῇ ἡμέρᾳ τοῦ κυρίου. (1 Cor. v. 5.)   3. πάντες γὰρ οἱ προφῆται καὶ ὁ νόμος ἕως Ἰωάννου ἐπροφήτευσαν.* (Matt. xi. 13.)   4. τίς ἐκ τῶν δύο ἐποίησεν τὸ θέλημα τοῦ πατρός; (Matt. xxi. 31.)   5. πάντες γὰρ ὡς προφήτην ἔχουσιν τὸν Ἰωάννην. (Matt. xxi. 26.)   6. καὶ αἰτήσας πινακίδιον ἔγραψεν. (Luke i. 63.)   7. Ἰησοῦς δὲ πλήρης πνεύματος ἁγίου ὑπέστρεψεν ἀπὸ τοῦ Ἰορδάνου. (Luke iv. 1.)   8. ὑπέστρεψεν μετὰ φωνῆς μεγάλης δοξάζων τὸν θεόν. (Luke xvii. 15.)   9. οὐδέποτε ἐλάλησεν οὕτως ἄνθρωπος. (John vii. 46.)   10. ὑμεῖς ἀεὶ τῷ πνεύματι τῷ ἁγίῳ ἀντιπίπτετε. (Acts vii. 51.)

XXVI.

§ 54. Verbs in -ω, in the aorist, subjunctive, middle.

ἵνα ἐγὼ καυχήσωμαι, *that I may boast.* (2 Cor. xi. 16.)
ὅσα ἂν αἰτήσῃ, *whatsoever thou mayst ask.* (John xi. 22.)
ὃ ἂν αἰτήσηται, *whatever she might ask.* (Matt. xiv. 7.)
ἐνδυσώμεθα, *let us put on.* (Rom. xiii. 12.)
τί ἐνδύσησθε, *what you shall put on.* (Matt. vi. 25.)
ἵνα αἰτήσωνται, *that they should ask for.* (Matt. xxvii. 20.)

§ 55. Adjectives not inflected like any of the preceding and of rare occurrence in the New Testament.

Rem. a. In Heb. vii. 3, and there only, we find ἀπάτωρ and ἀμήτωρ. Their inflection in classical Greek is like that of nouns of the third declension in -ωρ G. -ορος (§ 33 and *Rem. a*).

Rem. b. ἅρπαξ is inflected like nouns of the third declension with the G. ending γος (§ 27, *Rem. c*).

Rem. c. πένης is found only in the D. pl. πένησιν (1 Cor. ix. 9), and is inflected like nouns of the third declension with the G. in -ητος (§ 25 *Rem. b*).

---

* The T. R. reads προεφήτευσαν.

Rem. d. αὐτόχειρ is found only in the N. pl. (Acts xxvii. 19), and is inflected like χείρ (§ 33).

Rem. e. τετράπους is declinable in the masculine like πούς (§ 21), but in the N. T. occurs only in the neuter pl. τετράποδα G. -ων.

Rem. f. From νῆστις G. -ιος we have the A. pl. νήστεις in two passages (Matt. xv. 32, Mark viii. 3), but no other forms are found.

Rem. g. ἄρσην and ἄρρην are inflected like nouns of the third declension in -ην G. -ενος (§ 37, *Rem. a*).

Rem. h. μέλας (Rev. vi. 5, 12) has the A. sing. fem. μέλαιναν (Matt. v. 36), but no other forms are found.

Rem. i. ἑκών (1 Cor. ix. 17) has a feminine ἑκοῦσα (Rom. viii. 20) but no other forms. ἄκων (for ἀέκων = a privative and ἑκών) occurs once (1 Cor. ix. 17).

Rem. j. Ἑλληνίς and πατρίς are feminine and inflected like nouns of the third declension in -ις G. -ιδος (§ 24).

TRANSLATE

1. ἀγέλη χοίρων πολλῶν. (Matt. viii. 30.) 2. πολλοὶ τελῶναι καὶ ἁμαρτωλοί. (Matt. ix. 10.) 3. ὁ μὲν θερισμὸς πολύς, οἱ δὲ ἐργάται ὀλίγοι. (Matt. ix. 37.) 4. ἔχων κτήματα πολλά. (Matt. xix. 22.) 5. μετὰ δυνάμεως καὶ δόξης πολλῆς. (Matt. xxiv. 30.) 6. μετὰ δὲ πολὺν χρόνον ἔρχεται ὁ κύριος. (Matt. xxv. 19.) 7. γυναῖκες πολλαί. (Matt. xxvii. 55.) 8. καὶ πολὺ πλῆθος ἀπὸ τῆς Γαλιλαίας ἠκολούθησεν.* (Mark iii. 7.) 9. πολλοὺς γὰρ ἐθεράπευσεν. (Mark iii. 10.) 10. ὅπου οὐκ εἶχεν γῆν πολλήν. (Mark iv. 5.)

XXVII.

§ 56. Verbs in -ω, in the optative, passive and middle.

PRES. MID. εἰ βούλοιτο, *if he wished,* or *whether he was willing.* (Acts xxv. 20.)

AOR. PASS. πληθυνθείη, *may [it] be multiplied.* (1 Pet. i. 2.)

AOR. MID. εὐξαίμην ἄν, *I would pray,* or *I would [to God].* (Acts xxvi. 29.)

§57. The comparison of adjectives.

Rem. a. Most adjectives in -ος and -υς form their comparative and

---

* The T. R. reads ἠκολούθησαν.

superlative degrees by dropping s and adding τερος, -α, -ον and τατος, -α, -ον.

Rem. b. When the penult is short, adjectives in -ος compared as above lengthen ο to ω. Thus in 1 Cor. i. 25 we find σοφώτερον and not σοφότερον.

Rem. c. Adjectives in -ης shorten η into ε and add τερος, -α, -ον and -τατος, -α, -ον.

Rem. d. Adjectives in -ων shorten ω into ο and add εστερος, -α, -ον and εστατος, -α, -ον.

Rem. e. ταχύς and καλός take the endings ιων and ιστος, thus: ταχύς, ταχίων, τάχιστος; καλός, καλλίων, [κάλλιστος.]

Rem. f. The following are anomalous : —

Positive.	Comparative.	Superlative.
ἀγαθός,	κρείττων or -σσων, βελτίων,	κράτιστος.
κακός,	χείρων, ἥττων or -σσων.	
μέγας,	μείζων,	μέγιστος.
μικρός,	μικρότερος, ἐλάττων or -σσων,	ἐλάχιστος.
πολύς,	πλείων, n. πλεῖον or πλέον,	πλεῖστος.

Rem. g. μειζοτέραν (3 John 4) is a double comparative, ἐλαχιστοτέρῳ (Eph. iii. 8) a comparative formed from a superlative.

Rem. h. From the adverbs ἄνω, ἔσω, κάτω are formed the comparative adjectives ἀνώτερος, ἐσώτερος, κατώτερος.

TRANSLATE

1. σὺ πίστιν ἔχεις, κἀγὼ[1] ἔργα ἔχω. (James ii. 18.) 2. ἐπίστευσεν δὲ Ἀβραὰμ τῷ θεῷ. (James ii. 23.) 3. μεμέρισται ὁ Χριστός; (1 Cor. i. 13.) 4. ὁ ἔχων[2] τὰ ἑπτὰ πνεύματα τοῦ θεοῦ καὶ τοὺς ἑπτὰ ἀστέρας. (Rev. iii. 1.) 5. ἔρχομαι ταχύ.[3] (Rev. iii. 11.) 6. ἀγαπητοί, μὴ παντὶ πνεύματι πιστεύετε, ἀλλὰ δοκιμάζετε τὰ πνεύματα. (1 John iv. 1.) 7. ὅτι μὴ πεπίστευκεν εἰς τὸ ὄνομα τοῦ μονογενοῦς υἱοῦ τοῦ θεοῦ. (John iii. 18.) 8. καὶ πολλῷ[4] πλείους ἐπίστευσαν. (John iv. 41.) 9. τῷ σαββάτῳ[5] ἐθεράπευσεν ὁ Ἰησοῦς. (Luke xiii. 14.) 10. ἀστὴρ γὰρ ἀστέρος[6] διαφέρει ἐν δόξῃ. (1 Cor. xv. 41.)

[1] κἀγώ = καὶ ἐγώ.
[2] ὁ ἔχων, the [one] having, he who has.
[3] The neuter of adjectives is often used adverbially.
[4] See § 82, XVIII.   [5] See § 82, XXI.   [6] See § 82, II.

XXVIII.

§ 58. Verbs in -ὠ, in the present, imperative, passive and middle.

ἔγειρου, *arise (thou)*. (Luke viii. 54.)

προσευχέσθω, *let him pray.* (James v. 13.)

ἐγείρεσθε, *arise (ye)*. (Matt. xxvi. 46.)

δοκιμαζέσθωσαν, *let* [*them*] *be proved.* (1 Tim. iii. 10.)

§ 59. Numerals.

Rem. a. Of the cardinal numbers those which are declined are the first four, inflected as below, and the even hundreds (excepting ἑκατόν, *one hundred*), which are inflected like plural adjectives in -οι, -αι, -α.

Masc.	Fem.	Neut.	Masc., Fem., and Neut.
N. εἶς, *one*	μία	ἕν	N. δύο, *two*
G. ἑνός	μιᾶς	ἑνός	G. δύο
D. ἑνί	μιᾷ	ἑνί	D. δυσί(ν)
A. ἕνα	μίαν	ἕν	A. δύο

Masc. and Fem.	Neut.	Masc. and Fem.	Neut.
N. τρεῖς, *three*	τρία	N. τέσσαρες, *four*	τέσσαρα *
G. τριῶν	τριῶν	G. τεσσάρων	τεσσάρων
D. τρισί(ν)	τρισί(ν)	D. τέσσαρσι(ν)	τέσσαρσι(ν)
A. τρεῖς	τρία	A. τέσσαρας *	τέσσαρα *

Rem. b. The ordinal numbers end in *os* and are declined like adjectives in -ος, -η or -α, -ον.

TRANSLATE

1. προσευχέσθω ἵνα διερμηνεύῃ. (1 Cor. xiv. 13.) 2. ἐγείρεσθε, ἄγωμεν. (Mark xiv. 42.) 3. ἢ γὰρ τὸν ἕνα μισήσει καὶ τὸν ἕτερον ἀγαπήσει, ἢ ἑνὸς[1] ἀνθέξεται[2] καὶ τοῦ ἑτέρου[3] καταφρονήσει. (Matt. vi. 24.) 4. πόσῳ οὖν διαφέρει ἄνθρωπος προβάτου. (Matt. xii. 12.) 5. ἄνθρωπος εἶχεν δύο τέκνα. (Matt. xxi. 28.) 6. περιάγετε τὴν θάλασσαν καὶ τὴν ξηρὰν ποιῆσαι ἕνα προσήλυτον. (Matt. xxiii. 15.) 7. ἐκ τῶν τεσσάρων ἀνέμων. (Matt. xxiv. 31.) 8. καὶ ἤκουσα φωνὴν μίαν[4] ἐκ τῶν τεσσάρων κεράτων

---

* Tisch. reads τέσσερα and sometimes τέσσερας.

τοῦ θυσιαστηρίου τοῦ χρυσοῦ τοῦ ἐνώπιον τοῦ θεοῦ. (Rev. ix. 13.) 9. πόσους ἄρτους ἔχετε; (Matt. xv. 34.) 10. ἑπτά, καὶ ὀλίγα ἰχθύδια. (Matt. xv. 34.)

¹ See § 82, III.
² Whenever in compounds, or from the juxtaposition of distinct words, a smooth mute comes before a vowel with a rough breathing, the aspirate unites with the consonant to form the corresponding rough mute. See p. 4, *Rem. c.*
³ See § 82, VI.
⁴ εἰς is sometimes best translated by the indefinite article.

XXIX.

§ 60. Verbs in -ω, in the aorist, imperative, passive.

φυτεύθητι, *be (thou) planted.* (Luke xvii. 6.)
σταυρωθήτω, *let him be crucified.* (Matt. xxvii. 22.)
συνάχθητε, *gather yourselves together.* (Rev. xix. 17.)
[βουλευθήτωσαν, *let them be advised.*]

§ 61. The inflection of participles.

Rem. a. Those in -ος are inflected like adjectives in -ος, -α, -ον. See § 45, *Rem. a, d.*

Rem. b. Those in -ων and -ους have their feminine in -ουσα and their neuter in -ον. The masculine and neuter are declined like ἄρχων (§ 29), except that the neuter is subject to the rule in § 19, *Rem. e.*

Rem. c. Those in -ας, -εις and -υς have their feminines in -ασα -εισα and -υσα and their neuters in -αν, -εν and -υν. The masculines and neuters have their G. in -αντος, -εντος and -υντος and are declined like ἄρχων (§ 29), except that the neuters are subject to the rule in § 19, *Rem. e.*

Rem. d. Those in -ως have their feminine in -υια and their neuter in -ος. The masculine and neuter have their G. in -οτος and are declined similarly to the nouns in §§ 24 and 22. The only instance, among participles, of non-conformity to § 10, *Rem. b,* is συνειδυίης, Acts v. 2.

TRANSLATE

1. ἁγνίσθητι. (Acts xxi. 24.) 2. διανοίχθητι.¹ (Mark vii. 34.) 3. καὶ ᾄδουσιν τὴν ᾠδὴν Μωυσέως δούλου τοῦ θεοῦ καὶ τὴν ᾠδὴν τοῦ ἀρνίου. (Rev. xv. 3.) 4. καὶ ἡ πόλις οὐ χρείαν ἔχει τοῦ ἡλίου οὐδὲ τῆς σελήνης.

(Rev. xxi. 23.) 5. μὴ κλαῖε. (Rev. v. 5.) 6. καὶ ἤκουσα ὡς φωνὴν ὄχλου πολλοῦ καὶ ὡς φωνὴν ὑδάτων πολλῶν καὶ ὡς φωνὴν βροντῶν ἰσχυρῶν. (Rev. xix. 6.) 7. φοβήθητε τὸν θεόν. (Rev. xiv. 7.) 8. προσκυνήσατε τῷ ποιήσαντι τὸν οὐρανὸν καὶ τὴν γῆν. (Rev. xiv. 7.) 9. λῦσον τοὺς τέσσερας ἀγγέλους. (Rev. ix. 14.) 10. ἐξαλείψει [2] ὁ θεὸς πᾶν δάκρυον. (Rev. vii. 17.)

---

[1] See § 34, Rem. a. [2] See § 4, Rem. b.

XXX.

§ 62. Verbs in -ω, in the aorist, imperative, middle.

νίψαι, wash (thou). (Matt. vi. 17.)
προσκαλεσάσθω, let him call for. (James v. 14.)
ἐνωτίσασθε, give (ye) ear to. (Acts ii. 14.)
προσευξάσθωσαν, let them pray. (James v. 14.)

§ 63. The personal pronouns.

Rem. a. There are, in strictness, but two personal pronouns in N. T. Greek, ἐγώ, *I*, and σύ, *thou*, the place of the third being supplied (in the oblique cases, but seldom in the nominative) by the intensive αὐτός, *self*.

Rem. b. ἐγώ and σύ are inflected as follows : —

	Sing.	Pl.		Sing.	Pl.
N.	ἐγώ	ἡμεῖς	N.	σύ	ὑμεῖς
G.	ἐμοῦ, μοῦ	ἡμῶν	G.	σοῦ	ὑμῶν
D.	ἐμοί, μοί	ἡμῖν	D.	σοί	ὑμῖν
A.	ἐμέ, μέ	ἡμᾶς	A.	σέ	ὑμᾶς

Rem. c. αὐτός has three terminations, -ος, -η, -ο, and is declined after the manner of adjectives in -ος, -η, -ον.

TRANSLATE

1. ἀγιασθήτω τὸ ὄνομά σου. (Matt. vi. 9.) 2. τί ἐποίησέν σοι; πῶς ἤνοιξέν σοι τοὺς ὀφθαλμούς; (John ix. 26.) 3. τί πάλιν θέλετε ἀκούειν; (John ix. 27.) 4. λέγουσιν τῷ τυφλῷ [1] πάλιν, Σὺ τί λέγεις περὶ αὐτοῦ; (John ix. 17.) 5. ἐν ἁμαρτίαις σὺ ἐγεννήθης ὅλος, καὶ σὺ διδάσκεις ἡμᾶς; (John ix. 34.) 6. ἄγουσιν αὐτὸν πρὸς τοὺς Φαρισαίους, τόν ποτε τυφλόν. (John ix. 13.) 7. καὶ ὑμεῖς τὴν αὐτὴν [2] ἔννοιαν ὁπλίσασθε.

(1 Peter iv. 1.) 8. ὕπαγε νίψαι εἰς τὴν κολυμβήθραν τοῦ Σιλωάμ. (John ix. 7.) 9. τί με λέγεις ἀγαθόν; (Luke xviii. 19.) 10. ἔτι ἕν σοι λείπει. (Luke xviii. 22.)

¹ Supply ἀνθρώπῳ.
² αὐτός with the article has the force of 'the same.'

XXXI.

§ 64. Verbs in -ω, in the perfect, imperative, passive and middle.

> πεφίμωσο, be (thou) still. (Mark iv. 39.)
> [πεπειράσθω, let it be tried. — Arist. Vesp. 1129.]
> ἔρρωσθε, fare (ye) well. (Acts xv. 29.)
> [βεβουλεύσθωσαν, or -σθων, let them deliberate.]

§ 65. The Reflexive pronouns.

Rem. a. These are three in number, ἐμαυτοῦ, of myself, σεαυτοῦ, of thyself, and ἑαυτοῦ, of himself.

Rem. b. They are found only in the oblique cases, and in N. T. Greek the first two occur only in the masculine singular, the place of their plurals being supplied by the plural of ἑαυτοῦ.

Rem. c. ἑαυτοῦ has both masculine and feminine forms in both numbers. It is occasionally used for σεαυτοῦ.

Rem. d. The reflexives are declined (with the limitations above mentioned) like the intensive αὐτός (see § 63, *Rem. c*).

§ 66. The reciprocal pronoun ἀλλήλων, of each other, of one another.

Rem. In the N. T. the only forms are pl. G. ἀλλήλων, D. ἀλλήλοις, A. ἀλλήλους.

§ 67. Possessive pronouns.

Rem. a. From the genitives of the personal pronouns are formed the possessive adjective pronouns ἐμός, -ή, -όν, mine, ἡμέτερος, -α, -ον, ours, σός, -ή, -όν, thine, ὑμέτερος, -α, -ον, yours.

Rem. b. They are inflected like adjectives in -ος, -η or -α, -ον.

TRANSLATE

1. αὐτὸς¹ δὲ ὁ Ἰωάννης εἶχεν τὸ ἔνδυμα αὐτοῦ ἀπὸ τριχῶν² καμήλου καὶ ζώνην δερματίνην περὶ τὴν ὀσφὺν αὐτοῦ. (Matt. iii. 4.) 2. λέγει αὐτῷ ὁ Ἰησοῦς Πορεύου. (John iv. 50.) 3. κἀγὼ ἐὰν ὑψωθῶ ἐκ τῆς γῆς, πάντας ἑλκύσω πρὸς ἐμαυτόν. (John xii. 32.) 4. κἀγὼ ἀγαπήσω αὐτὸν καὶ ἐμφανίσω αὐτῷ ἐμαυτόν. (John xiv. 21.) 5. καὶ ὑπὲρ αὐτῶν ἐγὼ ἁγιάζω ἐμαυτόν. (John xvii. 19.) 6. προσέχετε οὖν ἑαυτοῖς. (Acts xx. 28.) 7. μισήσουσιν ἀλλήλους. (Matt. xxiv. 10.) 8. μὴ ἕνεκεν βρώματος κατάλυε τὸ ἔργον τοῦ θεοῦ. (Rom. xiv. 20.) 9. σὺ δὲ τί κρίνεις τὸν ἀδελφόν σου; (Rom. xiv. 10.) 10. ὁ ἐσθίων κυρίῳ ἐσθίει. (Rom. xiv. 6.)

¹ Intensive, ' himself.'　　　　　　² From θρίξ.

XXXII.

§ 68. Verbs in -ω, in the infinitive, passive and middle.

Pres. Pass. (and *Mid.*) θεραπεύεσθαι, *to be cured.* (Luke v. 15.)
Aorist Pass. πιστευθῆναι, *to be intrusted with.* (1 Thess. ii. 4.)
Aorist Mid. νίψασθαι, *to wash.* (John xiii. 10.)
Perf. Pass. (and *Mid.*) ἀπολελύσθαι, *to have been released.* (Acts xxvi. 32.)

§ 69. Demonstrative pronouns.

Rem. a. The principal ones are οὗτος, *this, this one,* and ἐκεῖνος, *that, that one.* The latter is declined like αὐτός (see § 63, *Rem. c*) : the former has for its nominatives οὗτος, αὕτη, τοῦτο, and οὗτοι, αὗται, ταῦτα, the remaining forms all beginning with τ and being inflected regularly like αὐτός.

Rem. b. In like manner are declined τοσοῦτος, -αύτη, -οῦτο, τοιοῦτος, -αύτη, -οῦτο, τηλικοῦτος, -αύτη, -οῦτο, and ἄλλος, -η, -ο.

§ 70. The relative pronoun ὅς.

Rem. Its forms in the N. sing. are ὅς, ἥ, ὅ, and it is inflected regularly like αὐτός.

§ 71. Interrogative and indefinite pronouns.

Rem. a. The interrogative τίς, neut. τί, and the indefinite pronoun of

OF THE NEW TESTAMENT.

the same form, are inflected like nouns of the third declension with the G. ending *νος* (see § 37), except that the neuters are subject to the rule in § 19, *Rem. e.*

Rem. b. The indefinite relative ὅστις, ἥτις, ὅ τι, *whoever, whatever,* (compounded of ὅς and τίς,) inflects both its component parts. In Matt. v. 25 occurs the secondary form ὅτου in place of the regular οὗτινος.

Rem. c. The indefinite δεῖνα, *such a one,* is found only in Matt. xxvi. 18.

TRANSLATE

1. οὐ γὰρ ὡς ὑμεῖς ὑπολαμβάνετε οὗτοι μεθύουσιν. (Acts ii. 15.)   2. ὁ δὲ Σίμων-καὶ αὐτὸς ἐπίστευσεν. (Acts viii. 13.)   3. ὁμοιωθήσεται* ἀνδρὶ φρονίμῳ, ὅστις[1] ᾠκοδόμησεν τὴν οἰκίαν αὐτοῦ ἐπὶ τὴν πέτραν. (Matt. vii. 24.)   4. πᾶσα φυτεία ἣν οὐκ ἐφύτευσεν ὁ πατήρ μου ὁ οὐράνιος ἐκριζωθήσεται. (Matt. xv. 13.)   5. ἀγαπήσεις τὸν πλησίον σου ὡς σεαυτόν. (Mark xii. 31.)   6. ὁ ἀγαθὸς ἄνθρωπος ἐκ τοῦ ἀγαθοῦ θησαυροῦ τῆς καρδίας αὐτοῦ προφέρει τὸ ἀγαθόν. (Luke vi. 45.)   7. ὁ δὲ Ἰησοῦς ἐπορεύετο σὺν αὐτοῖς. (Luke vii. 6.)   8. βλέπεις ταύτην τὴν γυναῖκα; (Luke vii. 44.)   9. τίνι οὖν ὁμοιώσω τοὺς ἀνθρώπους τῆς γενεᾶς ταύτης; (Luke vii. 31.)   10. ἥψατό μου[2] τίς. (Luke viii. 46.)

[1] In ὅστις it is implied that the man built upon the rock *because* he was prudent. Translate, "a man who, being prudent, built."

[2] See § 82, III.

XXXIII.

§ 72. Passive and middle participles of verbs in -ω, in the nominative singular masculine.

Pres. Pass. (and *Mid.*) ἐλεγχόμενος, *being reproved.* (Luke iii. 19.)
Aorist Pass. ἁγνισθείς, *having been purified.* (Acts xxi. 26.)
Aorist Mid. νιψάμενος, *having washed* (*myself*). (John ix. 11.)
Perf. Pass. (and *Mid.*) πεπαιδευμένος, *having been educated.* (Acts xxii. 3.)

Rem. On the inflection of the passive and middle participles see § 61, *Rem. a, c.*

§ 73. Contract verbs.

Rem. a. Verbs in -άω, -έω, and -όω are contracted in the present and

---

* Instead of ὁμοιωθήσεται the T. R. has ὁμοιώσω αὐτόν.

imperfect tenses, although there are a few exceptions to the rule. These contractions give rise to

ω from αω, αο, αου, εω, οω, οη,

ῳ from αοι,

α from αε, αη, αει (only in the infinitive active,)

ᾳ from αει, αη,

ει from εει, εε,

ου from εο, εου, οε, οει, οο, οου,

η from αει, εη,

ῃ from αει, εη,

οι from οει, οη, εοι, οοι.

Other contractions than these must be considered irregular. .

Rem. b. The second person singular of the present indicative passive and middle sometimes ends in σαι instead of ῃ

TRANSLATE

1. καὶ καθὼς θέλητε ἵνα ποιῶσιν ὑμῖν οἱ ἄνθρωποι, καὶ ὑμεῖς ποιεῖτε αὐτοῖς ὁμοίως. (Luke vi. 31.) 2. τί δέ με καλεῖτε κύριε, κύριε, καὶ οὐ ποιεῖτε ἃ λέγω; (Luke vi. 46.) 3. ἀγαπᾷ γὰρ τὸ ἔθνος ἡμῶν καὶ τὴν συναγωγὴν αὐτὸς ᾠκοδόμησεν ἡμῖν. (Luke vii. 5.) 4. καυχάσθω δὲ ὁ ἀδελφὸς ὁ ταπεινὸς [1] ἐν τῷ ὕψει αὐτοῦ. (James i. 9.) 5. ὑπόστρεφε εἰς τὸν οἶκόν σου. (Luke viii. 39.) 6. ἐν τῷ νόμῳ τί γέγραπται; [2] (Luke x. 26.) 7. πορεύου καὶ σὺ ποίει ὁμοίως. (Luke x. 37.) 8. καὶ διελογίζετο ἐν ἑαυτῷ λέγων Τί ποιήσω, [3] ὅτι οὐκ ἔχω ποῦ συνάξω τοὺς καρπούς μου; (Luke xii. 17.) 9. ἐφοβοῦντο τὸν λαόν. (Mark xi. 32.) 10. ὁ μὲν υἱὸς τοῦ ἀνθρώπου ὑπάγει καθὼς γέγραπται περὶ αὐτοῦ. (Mark xiv. 21.)

[1] When an attributive adjective stands after its noun, it regularly takes the article.
[2] See § 34, *Rem. a.*
[3] The subjunctive is used in deliberative questions.

XXXIV.

§ 74. Liquid verbs.

Rem. a. Those are called liquid verbs which, ending in ω, have one of the liquids (λ, μ, ν, ρ) as the last letter of the root.

Rem. b. More than two hundred of these, including compounds, are found in the N. T. The majority end in νω, while there are very few in -μω.

Rem. c. As a rule, these verbs do not have the tense characteristic (σ) in the future and aorist active and middle.

Rem. d. If the vowel before the liquid is long, in the future it is shortened, the diphthongs αι and ει becoming ᾰ and ε respectively; and one λ in verbs in -λλω being dropped.

Rem. e. In the aorist active the vowel before the liquid is uniformly long. If in the future it has been shortened (*Rem. d*), it is not always lengthened in the aorist to the form which it had in the present. The aorist and perfect passive and the perfect active retain the short vowel, although ε is often changed to α in verbs of two syllables.

Rem. f. In the future they are inflected like the present of contract verbs (see § 73), the ending ῶ having apparently come from -εσω through the intermediate -εω. The fut. indic. act. endings in full are *sing.* ῶ, εῖς, εῖ, *pl.* οῦμεν, εῖτε, οῦσιν.

Rem. g. The aorists active and middle are inflected regularly, except as above indicated.

Rem. h. Liquid and mute (and occasionally pure) verbs form the third person plural (and sometimes other persons both singular and plural) of the perf. and plup. pass. and mid. periphrastically, by prefixing, or else affixing, the N. of the perf. pass. part. to the pres. and imperf. tenses respectively of the verb εἰμί : *e. g.* γυναῖκές τινες αἱ ἦσαν τεθεραπευμέναι, *certain women who had been healed.* (Luke viii. 2.) Cf. § 44, *Rem. a.* and § 46, *Rem. a.*

TRANSLATE

1. ἐπιμενῶ δὲ Ἐφέσῳ ἕως τῆς πεντηκοστῆς. (1 Cor. xvi. 8.) 2. τότε ἠρώτησαν αὐτὸν ἐπιμεῖναι ἡμέρας τινάς.[1] (Acts x. 48.) 3. ἐπεμείναμεν αὐτοῦ ἡμέρας[1] ἑπτά. (Acts xxi. 4.) 4. μείνατε ὧδε καὶ γρηγορεῖτε μετ' ἐμοῦ. (Matt. xxvi. 38.) 5. ἔμεινεν δὲ Μαριὰμ σὺν αὐτῇ ὡσεὶ μῆνας[1] τρεῖς, καὶ ὑπέστρεψεν εἰς τὸν οἶκον αὐτῆς. (Luke i. 56.) 6. μεῖνον μεθ' ἡμῶν. (Luke xxiv. 29.) 7. καὶ ἐκεῖ ἔμειναν οὐ πολλὰς ἡμέρας.[1] (John ii. 12.) 8. ἐὰν τὰς ἐντολάς μου τηρήσητε, μενεῖτε ἐν τῇ ἀγάπῃ μου. (John xv. 10.) 9. τοῖς ἀγγέλοις αὐτοῦ ἐντελεῖται περὶ σοῦ. (Matt. iv. 6.) 10. ἡ ἐπαγγελία ἣν αὐτὸς ἐπηγγείλατο ἡμῖν. (1 John ii. 25.)

---

[1] See § 82, XXV.

XXXV.

§ 75. Duplicate or "second" tenses.

Rem. a. Sometimes in addition to certain of the regular tenses, but usually instead of them, many verbs have secondary forms.

Rem. b. The second aorist active ends in ον and is inflected like the imperfect active (§ 3). A second aorist active in -a (called the Alexandrian aorist) is occasionally met with, and also the Alexandrian ending οσαν for ον in the third person plural of the imperfect and second aorist active.

Rem. c. The second aorist passive ends in ην and is inflected like the first aorist passive (§ 38).

Rem. d. The second aorist middle ends in ομην and is inflected like the imperfect passive and middle (§ 32).

Rem. e. The second perfect active ends in a and is inflected like the first perfect active (§ 7).

Rem. f. The second pluperfect active ends in ειν and is inflected like the first pluperfect active (§ 9).

Rem. g. The second future passive ends in ησομαι and is inflected like the first future passive (§ 34).

Rem. h. The other modes are formed regularly from the indicative, the second aorist active and middle following the analogy of the present active and middle.

Rem. i. The root to which the endings of the second tenses are affixed is frequently not the exact root of the present, but a simpler form. Thus the second aorist active of φεύγω is not ἔφειγον (which is the form of the imperfect) but ἔφυγον (Matt. xxvi. 56). Sometimes the roots are altogether unlike, as in τρέχω (1 Cor. ix. 26), 2 aor. ἔδραμον (Matt. xxviii. 8).

TRANSLATE

1. πῶς φύγητε; (Matt. xxiii. 33.) 2. ἔφυγον ἀπὸ τοῦ μνημείου. (Mark xvi. 8.) 3. ἔφυγεν δὲ Μωυσῆς ἐν τῷ λόγῳ τούτῳ. (Acts vii. 29.) 4. ἐπυνθάνετο παρ' αὐτῶν ποῦ ὁ Χριστὸς γεννᾶται. (Matt. ii. 4.) 5. πυθόμενος ὅτι[1] ἀπὸ Κιλικίας. (Acts xxiii. 34.) 6. ἔδραμον[2] ἀπαγγεῖλαι τοῖς μαθηταῖς αὐτοῦ. (Matt. xxviii. 8.) 7. ἔτρεχον δὲ οἱ δύο ὁμοῦ. (John xx. 4.) 8. ἀπαγγείλατέ μοι. (Matt. ii. 8.) 9. ἀπήγγειλαν

πάντα. (Matt. viii. 33.) 10. ἀπήγγειλεν δὲ ὁ δεσμοφύλαξ τοὺς λόγους τούτους πρὸς τὸν Παῦλον. (Acts xvi. 36.)

¹ Supply in translation 'he was.'   ² See Rem. i.

XXXVI.

§ 76. Verbs in -μι.

Rem. a. About one hundred of the N. T. verbs end in μι, a very large proportion of which, however, are compounds, many of them of rare occurrence.

Rem. b. Their stems end either in η, ῡ, or (in a single instance) ω, lengthened from ε or ᾰ, ῠ and o, which are preserved in many of the forms.

Rem. c. δίδωμι and several verbs in -ημι have a reduplicated stem in the present and imperfect.

Rem. d. In the present, imperfect, and second aorist, the inflection of verbs in -μι is generally anomalous, chiefly from the absence of connecting vowels in the endings. Thus we have ἔθεντο (Acts v. 18) and not ἐθέοντο as the 2 aor. mid. of τίθημι. Such forms of these tenses as occur in the New Testament are given in the following sections.

Rem. e. Some verbs in -ω form the second aorist after the analogy of verbs in -μι.

§ 77. Forms of the verb δίδωμι (root δο), to give.*

ACTIVE.

Pres. Indic. sing. 1 δίδωμι (also διδῶ), 2 δίδως, 3 δίδωσι, pl. 3 διδόασιν; Subj. sing. 3 διδοῖ, pl. 3 διδῶσι; Imp. sing. 2 δίδου, 3 διδότω, pl. 2 δίδοτε; Inf. διδόναι; Part. διδούς (neut. διδοῦν in some MSS.).

Imperf. Indic. sing. 1 ἐδίδουν, 3 ἐδίδου, pl. 3 ἐδίδοσαν (in composition ἐδίδουν).

Aor. II. Indic. pl. 3 ἔδοσαν; Subj. sing. 1 δῶ, 2 δῷς, 3 δῷ and δοῖ, pl. 1 δῶμεν, 2 δῶτε, 3 δῶσι; Imp. sing. 2 δός, 3 δότω, pl. 2 δότε; Inf. δοῦναι; Part. δούς.

---

* In the forms given in this and succeeding sections, the prepositions of compound verbs are for the most part omitted. The numerals 1, 2, 3, indicate persons.

MIDDLE AND PASSIVE.

Pres. Indic. sing. 3 δίδοται, pl. 1 διδόμεθα; Inf. δίδοσθαι ; Part. διδόμενος.

Imperf. Indic. sing. 3 ἐδίδετο and ἐδίδοτο.

MIDDLE.

Aor. II. Indic. sing. 3 ἔδετο and ἔδοτο, pl. 2 ἔδοσθε, 3 ἔδοντο.

Rem. The peculiar form δώῃ or δῷ is Act. Aor. II. 3 sing. Subj. for δῷ or Opt. for δοίη according as editors place the ι subscript.

TRANSLATE

1. ὃς ἂν ἀπολύσῃ τὴν γυναῖκα αὐτοῦ, δότω αὐτῇ ἀποστάσιον. (Matt. v. 31.)   2. μὴ δῶτε τὸ ἅγιον τοῖς κυσίν. (Matt. vii. 6.)   3. δωρεὰν δότε. (Matt. x. 8.)   4. λέγουσιν αὐτῷ Τί οὖν Μωυσῆς ἐνετείλατο δοῦναι βιβλίον ἀποστασίου καὶ ἀπολῦσαι ; * (Matt. xix. 7.)   5. δῶμεν ἢ μὴ δῶμεν ; (Mark xii. 14.)   6. δὸς τούτῳ τόπον. (Luke xiv. 9.)   7. οὐδεὶς ἐδίδου αὐτῷ. (Luke xv. 16.)   8. ὁ πατήρ μου δίδωσιν ὑμῖν τὸν ἄρτον ἐκ τοῦ οὐρανοῦ τὸν ἀληθινόν. (John vi. 32.)   9. ὁ καταβαίνων ἐκ τοῦ οὐρανοῦ καὶ ζωὴν διδοὺς τῷ κόσμῳ. (John vi. 33.)   10. ἀπαγγελῶ τὸ ὄνομά σου τοῖς ἀδελφοῖς μου. (Heb. ii. 12.)

XXXVII.

§ 78. Forms of verbs in -ημι.

1. ἵστημι (root στα), *to place* or *station ;* Aor. 2, *to stand.*

ACTIVE.

Pres. Indic. sing. 1 ἵστημι, 3 ἵστησι and ἱστᾷ ; Subj. pl. 1 ἱστῶμεν ; Inf. ἱστάναι ; Part ἱστάς and ἱστῶν.

Aor. II. Indic. sing. 3 ἔστη, pl. 1 ἔστημεν, 2 ἔστητε, 3 ἔστησαν ; Subj. sing. 3 στῇ, pl. 2 στῆτε, 3 στῶσι ; Imp. sing. 2 στῆθι (and στα in composition), 3 στήτω, pl. 2 στῆτε ; Iuf. στῆναι ; Part στάς.

MIDDLE AND PASSIVE.

Pres. Indic. sing. 3 ἵσταται, pl. 3 ἵστανται ; Imp. sing. 2 ἵστασο ; Inf. ἵστασθαι ; Part. ἱστάμενος.

Imperf. Indic. sing. 3 ἵστατο, pl. 3 ἵσταντο.

---

* The T. R. adds αὐτήν.

2. τίθημι (root θε), *to put.*

ACTIVE.

Pres. Indic. sing. 1 τίθημι, 3 τίθησι, pl. 1 τίθεμεν, 3 τιθέασι ; Imp. sing. 2 τίθει, 3 τιθέτω ; Inf. τιθέναι ; part. τιθείς.

Imperf. Indic. sing. 1 ἐτίθουν, 3 ἐτίθει, pl. 3 ἐτίθεσαν, ἐτίθουν.

Aor. II. Subj. sing. 1 θῶ, 2 θῇς, 3 θῇ, pl. 3 θῶσι ; Imp. sing. 2 θές ; Inf. θεῖναι ; Part. θείς.

MIDDLE AND PASSIVE.

Pres. Indic. sing. 1 τίθεμαι, 3 τίθεται, pl. 2 τίθεσθε ; Imp. pl. 3 τιθέσθωσαν ; Inf. τίθεσθαι ; Part. τιθέμενος.

Imperf. Indic. sing. 3 ἐτίθετο, pl. 3 ἐτίθεντο.

Plup. Indic. pl. 3 ἐτέθειντο.

MIDDLE.

Aor. II. Indic. sing. 1 ἐθέμην, 2 ἔθου, 3 ἔθετο, pl. 2 ἔθεσθε, 3 ἔθεντο ; Subj. pl. 1 θώμεθα ; Imp. sing. 2 θοῦ, pl. 2 θέσθε ; Inf. θέσθαι ; Part. θέμενος.

TRANSLATE

1. ἐξίσταντο δὲ πάντες. (Acts ii. 12.)   2. ἔλεγον γὰρ ὅτι ἐξέστη. (Mark iii. 21.)   3. ἀνέστη τὸ κοράσιον καὶ περιεπάτει. (Mark v. 42.) 4. πάλιν γέγραπται Οὐκ ἐκπειράσεις κύριον[1] τὸν θεόν σου. (Matt. iv. 7.) 5. δεῖ πληρωθῆναι πάντα τὰ γεγραμμένα[2] ἐν τῷ νόμῳ Μωυσέως καὶ προφήταις[3] καὶ ψαλμοῖς[3] περὶ ἐμοῦ. (Luke xxiv. 44.)   6. ἑταῖρε, οὐκ ἀδικῶ σε· οὐχὶ δηναρίου[4] συνεφώνησάς[5] μοι; (Matt. xx. 13.)   7. συνελάλουν[6] πρὸς ἀλλήλους. (Luke iv. 36.)   8. κἀγὼ διατίθεμαι ὑμῖν καθὼς διέθετό μοι ὁ πατήρ μου βασιλείαν. (Luke xxii. 29.)   9. ἔτι αὐτοῦ λαλοῦντος[7] ἔρχεταί τις παρὰ τοῦ ἀρχισυναγώγου. (Luke viii. 49.) 10. μὴ φόβου, ἀλλὰ λάλει καὶ μὴ σιωπήσῃς. (Acts xviii. 9.)

---

[1] Proper names, when followed by a noun in apposition, do not take the article ; and κύριος is here used as a proper name.

[2] A labial (π, β, φ) before μ is changed into μ.

[3] Usually only the first of two or more nouns connected by καὶ and naturally grouped together has the article, when they agree in gender and number ; but if they differ in number, the article is very rarely omitted. In the present passage it may therefore be considered doubtful whether we should translate '*the prophets and the psalms*' or '*prophets and psalms.*'

[4] See § 82, X.

[5] ν is changed into μ before π, β, φ, but reappears whenever a vowel is interposed.

[6] ν before another liquid is changed into that liquid, reappearing when a vowel is interposed.

[7] See § 82, XI.

XXXVIII.

§ 79. Forms of verbs in -ημι, continued.

3. ἵημι, *to send.*

ACTIVE.

Pres. Indic. sing. 1 ἵημι, 3 ἵησι, pl. 1 ἵεμεν and ἵομεν, 2 ἵετε, 3 ἱᾶσι and ἱοῦσιν or ἵουσιν ; Subj. pl. 3 ἱῶσι ; Imp. sing. 3 ἱέτω, pl. 2 ἵετε ; Inf. ἱέναι ; Part. ἱείς and ἱών or ἱών.

Imperf. Indic. sing. 3 ἵεν.

Aor. II. Subj. sing. 1 ὦ, 3 ᾖ, pl. 1 ὦμεν, 2 ἦτε, 3 ὦσι ; Imp. sing. 2 ἕς, pl. 2 ἕτε ; Inf. εἶναι ; Part. εἵς.

MIDDLE AND PASSIVE.

Pres. Indic. sing. 3 ἵεται, pl. 3 ἵενται (ἵονται in the Cambridge MS.) ; Part. ἱέμενος.

Perf. Indic. pl. 3 ἕωνται.

4. φημί, *to say.*

ACTIVE.

Pres. Indic. sing. 1 φημί, 3 φησί, pl. 3 φασί.

Imperf. Indic. sing. 3 ἔφη.

5. πίμπρημι, *to burn.*

MIDDLE AND PASSIVE. — *Pres.* Inf. πίμπρασθαι.

6. ὀνίνημι, *to profit.*

MIDDLE. — *Aor. II.* Opt. sing. 1 ὀναίμην.

7. δύναμαι,* *to be able.*

Pres. Indic. sing. 1 δύναμαι, 2 δύνασαι, δύνῃ, 3 δύναται, pl. 1 δυνάμεθα, 2 δύνασθε, 3 δύνανται ; Subj. sing. 3 δύνηται, pl. 3 δύνωνται ; Opt. sing. 1 δυναίμην, pl. 3 δύναιντο ; Inf. δύνασθαι ; Part. δυνάμενος.

Imperf. Indic. sing. 3 ἠδύνατο, pl. 2 ἠδύνασθε, 3 ἠδύναντο.†

8. ἐπίσταμαι,* *to know, understand.*

Pres. Indic. sing. 1 ἐπίσταμαι, 3 ἐπίσταται, pl. 2 ἐπίστασθε, 3 ἐπίστανται ; Part. ἐπιστάμενος.

---

* Deponent.

† A few verbs have η instead of ε for their augment in the imperfect and aorist.

TRANSLATE

1. ἀκούετε καὶ συνίετε. (Matt. xv. 10.)   2. οὔπω νοεῖτε οὐδὲ συνίετε;
(Mark viii. 17.)   3. τότε διήνοιξεν αὐτῶν τὸν νοῦν τοῦ συνιέναι[1] τὰς
γράφας. (Luke xxiv. 45.)   4. ἡ δὲ προβιβασθεῖσα ὑπὸ τῆς μητρὸς
αὐτῆς Δός μοι, φησίν, ὧδε ἐπὶ πίνακι τὴν κεφαλὴν Ἰωάννου. (Matt. xiv.
8.)   5. οὗτος ἔφη, Δύναμαι καταλῦσαι τὸν ναὸν τοῦ θεοῦ καὶ διὰ τριῶν
ἡμερῶν οἰκοδομῆσαι. (Matt. xxvi. 61.)   6. καθώς φασίν τινες. (Rom.
iii. 8.)   7. λέγω γὰρ ὑμῖν ὅτι δύναται ὁ θεὸς ἐκ τῶν λίθων τούτων ἐγεῖραι
τέκνα τῷ Ἀβραάμ. (Matt. iii. 9.)   8. λέγουσιν αὐτῷ Δυνάμεθα. (Matt.
xx. 22.)   9. ὅσον χρόνον ἔχουσιν τὸν νυμφίον μετ᾽ αὐτῶν, οὐ δύνανται
νηστεύειν. (Mark ii. 19.)   10. καὶ ἐφοβήθησαν φόβον μέγαν.[2] (Mark
iv. 41.)

[1] See § 82, XII.   [2] See § 82, XXIII.

XXXIX.

§ 80. Forms of verbs in -υμι.

1. δείκνυμι, to show.

ACTIVE.
Pres. Indic. sing. 1 δείκνυμι, 3 δείκνυσι ; Part. δεικνύς.
MIDDLE AND PASSIVE.
Pres. Indic. pl. 3 δείκνυνται ; Inf. δείκνυσθαι ; Part. δεικνύμενος.

2. ἀμφιέννυμι, to put on, to clothe.

ACTIVE. — *Pres.* Indic. sing. 3 ἀμφιέννυσι.

3. ὑποζώννυμι, to undergird.

ACTIVE. — *Pres.* Part. ὑποζωννύς.

4. ἀπόλλυμι, to destroy.

MIDDLE AND PASSIVE.
Pres. Indic. sing. 1 ἀπόλλυμαι, 3 ἀπόλλυται, pl. 1 ἀπολλύμεθα ; Part.
ἀπολλύμενος.
(MID. *Aor. II.* ὠλόμην, regular.)

5. ῥήγνυμι, to break.

MIDDLE AND PASSIVE.
Pres. Indic. pl. 3 ῥήγνυνται. *Imperf.* Indic. sing. 3 ἐρρήγνυτο.

6. δύμι, *to sink, go down :* pres. in actual use, δύνω.

ACTIVE. — *Aor. II.* sing. 3 ἔδυ.

7. κρεμάννυμι, *to hang up.*

MIDDLE AND PASSIVE.

Pres. Indic. sing. 3 κρέμαται, pl. 3 κρέμανται ; Part. κρεμάμενος, — following the analogy of verbs in -ημι.

Imperf. Indic. sing. 3 ἐκρέματο, ἐκρέμετο.

8. σβέννυμι, *to quench.*

ACTIVE.

Pres. Imp. pl. 2 σβέννυτε.

MIDDLE AND PASSIVE.

Pres. Indic. sing. 3 σβέννυται, pl. 3 σβέννυνται.

9. συναναμίγνυμι, *to mix up with.*

MIDDLE AND PASSIVE.

Pres. Imp. pl. 2 συναναμίγνυσθε ; Inf. συναναμίγνυσθαι.

10. ὄμνυμι, *to swear.*

ACTIVE. — *Pres.* Inf. ὀμνύναι.

§81. **Inflection of the verbs** εἰμί, *to be,* **and** εἶμι, *to go.*

1. εἰμί.

Pres. Ind. sing. 1 εἰμί, 2 εἶ, 3 ἐστί, pl. 1 ἐσμέν, 2 ἐστέ, 3 εἰσί ; Subj. sing. 1 ὦ, 2 ᾖς, 3 ᾖ, pl. 1 ὦμεν, 2 ἦτε, 3 ὦσι ; Opt. sing. 2 εἴης, 3 εἴη ; Imp. sing. 2 ἴσθι, 3 ἔστω, ἤτω, pl. 3 ἔστωσαν ; Inf. εἶναι ; Part. ὤν.

Imperf. Indic. sing. 1 ἤμην, 2 ἦς, ἦσθα, 3 ἦν, pl. 1 ἦμεν, ἤμεθα, 2 ἦτε, 3 ἦσαν.

Fut. Indic. sing. 1 ἔσομαι, 2 ἔσῃ, 3 ἔσται, pl. 1 ἐσόμεθα, 2 ἔσεσθε, 3 ἔσονται ; Inf. ἔσεσθαι ; Part. ἐσόμενος.

2. εἶμι (in the N. T. found only in composition).

Pres. Indic. pl. 3 ἴασι ; Imp. sing. 2 ἴθι in the Vatican MS. ; Inf. ἰέναι ; Part. ἰών.

Imperf. Indic. sing. 3 ᾔει, pl. 3 ᾖεσαν.

TRANSLATE

1. μὴ συσχηματίζεσθε[1] τῷ αἰῶνι τούτῳ. (Rom. xii. 2.) 2. πάντα γὰρ ὑμῶν[2] ἐστιν.[3] (1 Cor. iii. 21.) 3. καὶ οὐκ ἐστὲ ἑαυτῶν.[2] (1 Cor. vi. 19.) 4. τίνος τῶν ἑπτὰ ἔσται γυνή; (Matt. xxii. 28.) 5. εἰ δέ τις

πνεῦμα Χριστοῦ οὐκ ἔχει, οὗτος οὐκ ἔστιν αὐτοῦ.[1] (Rom. viii. 9.) 6.
ἠκούσατε τῆς βλασφημίας · [4] τί ὑμῖν φαίνεται; (Mark. xiv. 64.) 7. σὺ
εἶ ὁ βασιλεὺς τῶν Ἰουδαίων; (Mark. xv. 2.) 8. οὗτός ἐστιν ὁ υἱός μου
ὁ ἀγαπητός. (Matt. xvii. 5.) 9. εἰ ἐκ τοῦ κόσμου ἦτε, ὁ κόσμος ἂν τὸ
ἴδιον ἐφίλει.[5] (John xv. 19.) 10. ἐξέδυσαν αὐτὸν τὴν χλαμύδα.[6] (Matt.
xxvii. 31.)

[1] When σύν in composition is followed by ζ or by σ and another consonant, it may
either retain its full form or be shortened to συ.
[2] See § 82, IV.   [4] See § 82, V.   [6] See § 82, XXIV.
[3] See § 82, I.   [5] See § 3, Rem. a.

XL.

§ 82. Rules of Syntax.

I. A neuter plural may be the subject of a singular verb.

II. Verbs implying separation and source are followed by the genitive.

III. All words expressing or implying a part or action upon a part of
anything are followed by a genitive of the whole.

IV. The genitive (and sometimes the dative) is used to denote possession.

V. Verbs of sense, except those of sight, may govern the genitive.

VI. Many verbs denoting operations of the mind govern the genitive.

VII. Verbs of accusing, convicting, etc., are followed by a genitive of
the person and an accusative of the crime.

VIII. Certain verbs implying a noun govern the genitive.

IX. Words signifying plenty and want are followed by the genitive.

X. The price of a thing is put in the genitive.

XI. A noun or a pronoun and a participle may stand in the genitive,
to denote the time or some other circumstance of an action. This is
called the *genitive absolute*.

XII. The genitive of the neuter article with an infinitive is often used
to denote purpose.

XIII. The comparative degree usually governs the genitive, except
when followed by ἤ.

XIV. The instrument with which and the means by which anything
is done are put in the dative.

XV. A noun used to denote the mode or manner of an action is put in the dative, with or without a preposition.

XVI. The dative is used to denote that with reference to which, in accordance with which, or on account of which, something is or takes place.

XVII. Words denoting likeness or similarity are followed by the dative.

XVIII. The dative is used with comparatives and verbs implying comparison, to indicate to what extent one thing exceeds or falls short of another.

XIX. Verbs signifying to contend with, to use, and sometimes those of participating in, are followed by the dative.

XX. The dative is sometimes used after passive verbs to denote the agent.

XXI. The dative (very rarely the genitive) is used to denote the time at which (sometimes during which) a thing takes place, and occasionally the place where.

XXII. An accusative case may be the subject of an infinitive.

XXIII. Many verbs are followed by an accusative of kindred signification.

XXIV. Some verbs take two accusatives, one of the person and the other of the thing.

XXV. Duration of time and extent of space are put in the accusative.

TRANSLATE

1. βούλομαι οὖν προσεύχεσθαι τοὺς ἄνδρας [1] ἐν παντὶ τόπῳ. (1 Tim. ii. 8.) 2. καὶ κατηγόρουν αὐτοῦ [2] οἱ ἀρχιερεῖς πολλά. [3] (Mark xv. 3.) 3. Γαλλίωνος [3] δὲ ἀνθυπατεύοντος τῆς Ἀχαίας [4] κατεπέστησαν ὁμοθυμαδὸν οἱ Ἰουδαῖοι τῷ Παύλῳ. (Acts xviii. 12.) 4. ἰδοὺ πεπληρώκατε τὴν Ἰερουσαλὴμ τῆς διδαχῆς [5] ὑμῶν. (Acts v. 28.) 5. ἐσφραγίσθητε τῷ πνεύματι [6] τῆς ἐπαγγελίας τῷ ἁγίῳ. (Eph. 1. 13.) 6. πᾶσα δὲ γυνὴ προσευχομένη ἢ προφητεύουσα ἀκατακαλύπτῳ τῇ κεφαλῇ [7] καταισχύνει τὴν κεφαλὴν ἑαυτῆς. (1 Cor. xi. 5.) 7. εἰ γὰρ καὶ τῇ σαρκὶ [8] ἄπειμι ἀλλὰ τῷ πνεύματι [8] σὺν ὑμῖν εἰμί. (Col. ii. 5.) 8. ὅμοιοι αὐτῷ [9] ἐσόμεθα. (1 John iii. 2.) 9. ἀλλ' οὐκ ἐχρησάμεθα τῇ ἐξουσίᾳ [10] ταύτῃ. (1 Cor. ix. 12.) 10. εὑρέθην [11] τοῖς [12] ἐμὲ μὴ ζητοῦσιν. (Rom. x. 20.)

[1] Rule XXII. [2] Rule VII. [3] Rule XI. [4] Rule VIII. [5] Rule IX.
[6] Rule XIV. [7] Rule XV. [8] Rule XVI. [9] Rule XVII. [10] Rule XIX.
[11] Aor. I. pass. of εὑρίσκω, an irregular verb. [12] Rule XX.

VOCABULARY.

A.

'Ααρών, ὁ, Aaron.

'Αβραάμ, ὁ, Abraham.

ἄβυσσος, ου, ἡ, an abyss.

ἀγαθός, ή, όν, adj., good.

ἀγαπάω, to love.

ἀγάπη, ης, ἡ, love.

ἀγαπητός, ή, όν, adj., beloved.

ἄγγελος, ου, ὁ, a messenger, an angel.

ἀγέλη, ης, ἡ, a herd.

ἀγιάζω, to make clean or holy, to hallow.

ἅγιος, ία, ιον, adj., holy.

ἁγνίζω, to purify.

ἀγοράζω, to buy.

'Αγρίππας, α, ὁ, Agrippa.

ἄγω, to lead, to bring, to go.

ἀδελφή, ῆς, ἡ, a sister.

ἀδελφός, οῦ, ὁ, a brother.

ἀδικέω, to do injustice, to hurt, to harm.

ᾄδω, to sing.

ἀεί, adv., ever, always.

ἀήρ, ἀέρος, ὁ, air.

αἰδώς, όος, οῦς, ἡ, modesty, reverence.

αἰτέω, to ask, to ask for.

αἰών, ῶνος, ὁ, an age ; ὁ αἰών, the age, the world.

ἀκατακάλυπτος, ὁ, ἡ, adj., unveiled, uncovered.

ἀκολουθέω, to follow.

ἀκούω, to hear.

ἀλήθεια, ας, ἡ, truth.

ἀληθινός, ή, όν, adj., true.

ἀλλά (an adversative particle, stronger than δέ), but, yet.

ἀλλήλων, of one another.

ἅλων, ωνος, ἡ, a threshing-floor.

ἁμαρτία, ας, ἡ, sin.

ἁμαρτωλός, οῦ, ὁ, ἡ, adj., sinful, subst., a sinner.

ἀμπελών, ῶνος, ὁ, a vineyard.

ἄν, a particle usually calling for no translation, but serving to give an air of uncertainty or indefiniteness to the words with which it is connected. It may sometimes be rendered "perchance." After relative pronouns it is equivalent to the English termination -ever, e. g. ὃς ἄν, whoever : with verbs, it is often equivalent to the auxiliary would.

ἀναβαίνω, to go up.

ἀνάγω, to lead up ; mid. and pass., to set sail.

ἀνακρίνω, to examine.

ἀναχωρέω, to go back, to withdraw.

ἄνεμος, ου, ὁ, wind.

ἀνέχομαι, to bear with.

ἀνήρ, ἀνδρός, ὁ, a man, a husband.

ἄνθρωπος, ου, ὁ, a human being, a man.

ἀνθυπατεύω, to be proconsul.

ἀνθύπατος, ου, ὁ, a proconsul.

ἀνίστημι, to raise up ; aor. 2, to rise up.

ἀνοίγω, to open.

ἀντέχομαι, to cleave to.

ἀντί (with gen.), over against, in exchange for, for.

ἀντιπίπτω, to resist.

ἀπαγγέλλω, to announce, to tell, to report.

ἀπάγχω, to strangle (to death).
ἄπειμι, to be absent.
ἀπέναντι, adv., in the presence of.
ἄπιστος, ον, adj., without faith, unbelieving.
ἀπό (with gen.), from.
Ἀπολλώς, ώ, ὁ, Apollos.
ἀπολύω, to free from, to free one's self from, to put away.
ἀπονίπτω, to wash off, to wash.
ἀποστάσιον, ου, τό, a divorce, a bill of divorce.
ἀπόστολος, ου, ὁ, an apostle.
ἅπτω, to touch.
ἀρνίον, ου, τό, a lamb.
ἄρτι, adv., now, just now.
ἄρτος, ου, ὁ, a loaf of bread, bread, food.
ἀρχιερεύς, έως, ὁ, a chief priest.
ἀρχισυνάγωγος, ου, ὁ, a ruler of a synagogue.
ἄρχομαι, to begin.
ἄρχων, ὁ, a ruler.
ἀστήρ, έρος, ὁ, a star.
ἄστρον, ου, τό, a star.
αὐτός, ἡ, ὁ, self; in oblique cases, him, her, it.
αὐτοῦ, adv., there.
ἀφορίζω, to separate.
ἄφρων, ον, adj., senseless, foolish.
Ἀχαΐα, ας, ἡ, Achaia.

B.

βάθος, εος, ους, τό, depth.
βάλλω, to cast, to put, to pour.
βαρέω, to weigh down.
Βαρνάβας, α, ὁ, Barnabas.
βασανίζω, to torment.
βασιλεία, ας, ἡ, a reign, a kingdom.
βασιλεύς, έως, ὁ, a king.
βασιλεύω, to reign.
βιβλίον, ου, τό, a writing.
βλασφημέω, to blaspheme.
βλασφημία, ας, ἡ, blasphemy.

βλέπω, to look, to see.
βότρυς, υος, ὁ, a bunch of grapes.
βούλομαι, to will, wish, desire.
βοῦς, οός, ὁ, ἡ, an ox or cow.
βραδύς, εῖα, ύ, adj., slow.
βροντή, ῆς, ἡ, thunder.
βρυγμός, οῦ, ὁ, a gnashing (of the teeth).
βρύχω, to gnash (the teeth).
βρῶμα, ατος, τό, food.
βρῶσις, εως, ἡ, food.

Γ.

γάλα, ακτος, τό, milk.
Γαλιλαία, ας, ἡ, Galilea.
Γαλλίων, ωνος, ὁ, Gallio.
γαμέω, to marry.
γάρ, conj., for.
γαστήρ, τέρος, τρός, ἡ, the belly.
γενεά, ᾶς, ἡ, a generation.
γεννάω, to beget, to bring forth; pass., to be born.
γῆ, γῆς, ἡ, land, earth.
γῆρας, αος, ως, τό, old age.
γίνομαι, to become, to be.
γλῶσσα, ης, ἡ, the tongue.
γόνυ, γόνατος, τό, the knee.
γραμματεύς, έως, ὁ, a scribe.
γραφή, ῆς, ἡ, a writing, a scripture.
γράφω, to write.
γρηγορέω, to watch.
γυνή, γυναικός, ἡ, a woman, a wife.
γυνὴ χήρα, a widow-woman, a widow.

Δ.

δάκρυον, ου, τό, a tear.
δέ, conj., but, and; δὲ καί (emphatic), and also.
δεῖ, it is necessary, it must be.
δένδρον, ου, τό, a tree.
δερμάτινος, η, ον, adj., leathern.
δεσμοφύλαξ, ακος, ὁ, a jailer.
δεσπότης, ου, ὁ, a master.
δέχομαι, to receive.
δηνάριον, ίου, τό, a denarius.

διά (with gen. and acc.), through, during, in, on account of.

διαλέγομαι, to discourse.

διαλογίζομαι, to reason.

διανοίγω, to open.

διαστρέφω, to turn away (any one).

διατίθημι, to appoint, to assign.

διαφέρω, to differ from, to be worth more than.

διδάσκω, to teach.

διδαχή, ῆς, ἡ, teaching.

δίδωμι, to give.

διερμηνεύω, to interpret.

δικαιοσύνη, ης, ἡ, justice, righteousness.

διορύσσω, to dig through, to break through.

Διοτρεφής, έος, οῦς, ὁ, Diotrephes.

διώκω, to pursue, to persecute.

δοκιμάζω, to consider worth, to try, to test.

δόξα, ης, ἡ, glory.

δοξάζω, to give glory to, to glorify.

δουλεύω, to serve, to be in servitude.

δοῦλος, ου, ὁ, a servant.

δράκων, οντος, ὁ, a dragon.

δύναμαι, to be able.

δύναμις, εως, ἡ, power, might, strength.

δύο, two.

δωρεάν, adv., gratuitously, freely.

E.

ἐάν (εἰ and ἄν), if, if perchance.

ἑαυτοῦ, of himself.

ἐγείρω, to raise up; mid., to arise.

ἐγκόπτω, to hinder.

ἐγώ, I.

ἔθνος, ους, τό, a nation.

εἰ, conj., if; εἰ μή, except.

εἰμί, to be.

εἰς (with acc.), to, into, in, for, at.

εἷς, μία, ἕν, one.

ἐκ (with gen.), from, because of, on account of; before a vowel, ἐξ.

ἐκδύω, to strip.

ἐκεῖ, adv., there.

ἐκπειράζω, to make trial of, to tempt.

ἐκπίπτω, to fail.

ἐκριζόω, to root up.

ἐλάσσων or -ττων, ον, adj. (comparative of μικρός), less, younger.

ἑλκύω, to draw.

Ἑλλάς, άδος, ἡ, Hellas, Greece.

ἐλπίς, ίδος, ἡ, hope.

ἐμαυτοῦ, of myself.

ἐμβλέπω, to look at, to consider; (with or without εἰς).

ἔμπροσθεν, adv. and prep., before.

ἐμφανίζω, to manifest.

ἐν (with dat.), in, by, among.

ἔνδυμα, ατος, τό, clothing.

ἕνεκεν (with gen.), on account of, for the sake of.

ἔννοια, ας, ἡ, thought, purpose.

ἐντέλλομαι, fut. τελοῦμαι, to command.

ἐντολή, ῆς, ἡ, a command.

ἐνώπιον (with gen.), in the presence of, before.

ἐξαλείφω, to blot out, to wipe away.

ἐξίστημι, to astonish; mid. and aor. 2 act., to be astonished, to be beside one's self.

ἐξουσία, ας, ἡ, power, authority, right.

ἔξωθεν, adv., from without. τὸ ἔξωθεν, the outside.

ἐπαγγελία, ας, ἡ, a promise.

ἐπαγγέλλομαι, to promise.

ἐπί (with gen., dat. and acc.), on, upon, towards, at, before (i. e. into the presence of).

ἐπίθεσις, εως, ἡ, a placing on, a laying on.

ἐπιμένω, fut. μενῶ, to remain.

ἐπιστρέφω, to turn towards, to turn.

ἐπονομάζω, to name.

ἑπτά, seven.

ἐργάτης, ου, ὁ, a workman, a laborer.

ἔργον, ου, τό, work.

ἔρις, ιδος, ἡ, strife.
ἔριφος, ου, ὁ, ἡ, a kid, a young goat.
Ἑρμογένης, εος, ους, ὁ, Hermogenes.
ἔρχομαι, to come.
ἐρωτάω, to ask.
ἐσθίω, to eat.
ἔσωθεν, adv., from within. τὸ
  ἔσωθεν, the inside.
ἑταῖρος, ου, ὁ, a companion, a friend.
ἕτερος, a, ον, adj., other.
ἔτι, adv., more, still.
ἑτοιμάζω, to prepare.
εὐαγγέλιον, ου, τό, good news, the
  gospel.
εὑρίσκω, to find.
Ἔφεσος, ου, ἡ, Ephesus.
ἔχω, to have, to hold, to consider.
ἕως, adv., until.

Z.

ζάω, fut. ζήσω and ζήσομαι, to live.
Ζεβεδαῖος, ου, ὁ, Zebedee.
ζητέω, to seek.
ζωή, ῆς, ἡ, life.
ζώνη, ης, ἡ, a girdle.

H.

ἤ, or ; ἤ — ἤ, either — or.
ἡγεμών, όνος, ὁ, a governor.
ἡδέως, adv., gladly.
Ἡλίας, ου, ὁ, Elias, Elijah.
ἥλιος, ου, ὁ, the sun.
ἡμεῖς (pl. of ἐγώ) we.
ἡμέρα, ας, ἡ, a day.
Ἡρώδης, ου, ὁ, Herod.
Ἡρωδιάς, άδος, ἡ, Herodias.
Ἡσαΐας, ου, ὁ, Esaias, Isaiah.
ἥσσων or -ττων, ον, adj. (compar.
  of κακός), worse.

Θ.

θάλασσα, ης, ἡ, a sea, a lake.
θέλημα, ατος, τό, will.
θέλω, to will, wish, desire.
θεός, οῦ, ὁ, a god, God.

θεραπεύω, to heal, to cure.
θερισμός, οῦ, ὁ, a harvest.
θηρίον, ου, τό, a wild beast, a beast.
θησαυρίζω, to treasure up.
θησαυρός, οῦ, ὁ, treasure, wealth.
θρίξ, G. τριχός, ἡ, a hair.
θυγατήρ, τέρος, τρός, ἡ, a daughter.
θυσιαστήριον, ου, τό, an altar.

I.

ἴδιος, ία, ον, adj., own, one's own.
ἰδού, interj., behold !
Ἱερουσαλήμ, Jerusalem.
Ἰησοῦς, οῦ, ὁ, Jesus.
ἱμάς, άντος, ὁ, a thong, a strap, a
  latchet.
ἵνα, that, in order that, to.
Ἰορδάνης, ου, ὁ, the Jordan.
Ἰουδαία, ας, ἡ, Judæa.
Ἰουδαῖος, α, ον, adj., Jewish ; subst.
  masc., a Jew.
Ἰούδας, α, ὁ, Judas, Judah.
ἰσχυρός, ά, όν, adj., mighty.
ἰχθύδιον, ου, τό, a small fish.
ἰχθύς, ύος, ὁ, a fish.
Ἰωάννης, ου, ὁ, John.
Ἰωνᾶς, ᾶ, ὁ, Jonah, Jonas.
Ἰωσήφ, ὁ, Joseph.

K.

καθαρίζω, to purify, to cleanse.
καθώς, adv., as.
καί, conj., and, even, also.
κακόω, to maltreat.
καλέω, to call.
καλός, ή, όν, adj., beautiful, good.
καλῶς, adv., well.
κάμηλος, ου, ὁ, ἡ, a camel.
κἄν (a contraction of καὶ ἐάν), even
  if, though.
καρδία, ας, ἡ, the heart.
καρπός, οῦ, ὁ, fruit.
κατά (with gen. and acc.), down,
  according to.
καταβαίνω, to go or come down.

καταισχύνω, to bring shame upon, to dishonor, to disgrace.
καταλύω, to destroy.
κρταρτίζω, to prepare.
κατασείω, to wave, to beckon.
καταφρονέω, to despise.
κατεργάζομαι, to work out, to produce.
κατεφίστημι, to stand up against, to rush upon.
κατέχω, to hold.
κατηγορέω, to accuse, to accuse of.
καυχάομαι, to boast.
κέρας, ατος, τό, a horn.
κεφαλή, ῆς, ἡ, the head.
κήρυγμα, ατος, τό, preaching.
κηρύσσω, to proclaim, to preach.
Κιλικία, ας, ἡ, Cilicia.
κλαίω, to weep.
κλαυθμός, οῦ, ὁ, a weeping.
κλείς, κλειδός, ἡ, a key.
κλέπτης, ου, ὁ, a thief.
κλέπτω, to steal.
κλίνω, to recline.
κόκκος, ου, ὁ, a grain, a seed.
κολυμβήθρα, ας, ἡ, a swimming-place, a pool.
κοράσιον, ίου, τό, a girl, a maiden.
κόσμος, ου, ὁ, order, the world.
κρατέω, to lay hold of, hold, retain.
κρέας, ατος, τό, meat, flesh; pl. κρέατα, contr. κρέα.
κρείσσων, or -ττων, ον, adj. (comp. of ἀγαθός), better.
κρημνός, οῦ, ὁ, a steep place.
κρίνω, to judge.
Κρίσπος, ου, ὁ, Crispus.
κτῆμα, ατος, τό, a possession.
κύριος, ου, ὁ, a lord, a master.
κύων, G. κυνός, ὁ, ἡ, a dog.
κώμη, ης, ἡ, a village.
Κῶς, acc. Κῶν, ἡ, [the island of] Cos or Co.

Λ.

λαλέω, to speak, to talk.
λαμβάνω, to receive.
λάμπω, to shine, to give light.
λαός, οῦ, ὁ, a people.
λατρεύω, to serve.
λέγω, to say, to call.
λείπω, to leave, to lack, to be wanting.
λεπρός, οῦ, ὁ, a leper.
Λευείς (or Λευίς), acc. Λευείν (or Λευίν), ὁ, Levi.
λίθος, ου, ὁ, a stone.
λίμνη, ης, ἡ, a lake.
λόγος, ου, ὁ, a word.
Λυδία, ας, ἡ, Lydia.
λύω, to loosen.
Λώτ, ὁ, Lot.

Μ.

μαθητής, οῦ, ὁ, a learner, a disciple.
μαλακία, ας, ἡ, weakness, disease.
μανθάνω, to learn.
Μαριάμ, ἡ, Mary.
μαρτυρέω, to bear witness, to testify.
μαρτυρία, ας, ἡ, testimony.
μάρτυς, υρος, ὁ, a witness.
μέγας, μεγάλη, μέγα, adj., great.
μεθύω, to be drunk.
μείζων, ον, adj. (comp. of μέγας), greater, older.
μέν, conjunctive particle, indeed.
μένω, to remain, to abide.
μερίζω, to divide.
μετά (with gen. and acc.), with, after.
μετανοέω, to change one's mind, to repent.
μή, not; also an interrogative particle.
μήν, μηνός, ὁ, a month.
μήτε — μήτε, neither — nor.
μήτηρ, τρός, ἡ, a mother.
μισέω, to hate.
μνημεῖον, ου, τό, a tomb, a sepulchre.
μνημονεύω, to remember.
μονογενής, adj., only begotten.
μόνος, η, ον, adj., only, alone.
Μωϋσῆς, έως, ὁ, Moses.

N.

ναός, οῦ, ὁ, a temple.

νεφέλη, ης, ἡ, a cloud.

νηστεύω, to fast.

νίπτω, to wash (some part of the body).

νιπτήρ, ῆρος, ὁ, a wash-basin.

νοέω, to perceive.

νόμος, ου, ὁ, a law.

νόσος, ου, ἡ, sickness, disease.

νοῦς, νοός, ὁ, mind.

νύμφη, ης, ἡ, a bride.

νυμφίος, ου, ὁ, a bridegroom.

νῦν, now.

Ξ.

ξηρός, ά, όν, adj., dry; ξηρά (γῆ being understood), dry land, land.

Ο.

ὁ, ἡ, τό, the.

ὁδός, οῦ, ἡ, a road, a way.

ὁδούς, ὁδόντος, ὁ, a tooth.

οἰκία, ας, ἡ, a house.

οἰκοδομέω, to build.

οἶκος, ου, ὁ, a house.

οἰνοπότης, ου, ὁ, a wine-bibber.

οἶνος, ου, ὁ, wine.

ὀλίγος, η, ον, adj., little; pl. few.

ὅλος, η, ον, adj., whole, altogether.

ὁμοθυμαδόν, adv., with one accord.

ὅμοιος, α, ον, adj., like.

ὁμοιόω, to make like, to liken, to compare.

ὁμοίως, adv., in like manner.

ὁμοῦ, adv., together.

ὄνομα, ατος, τό, a name.

ὁπλίζω, to arm.

ὅπου, adv., where.

ὀργή, ῆς, ἡ, anger, wrath.

ὀργίζω, to be enraged.

ὁρμάω, to rush.

ὄρος, εος, ους, τό, a mountain, a hill.

ὅς, ἥ, ὅ, who, which; ὃς ἄν, whoever.

ὅσος, η, ον, how great, as great as, how long, as long as.

ὀστέον (contr. ὀστοῦν), ου, τό, a bone.

ὅστις, ἥτις, ὅ τι, whoever, whatever.

ὀσφύς, ύος, ἡ, the loins.

ὅταν, adv. (ὅτε and ἄν), when, when perchance.

ὅτε, adv., when.

ὅτι, conj., that, because.

οὐ (οὐκ before smooth and οὐχ before aspirated vowels), not. (οὐ is used in the statement of negative facts, μή of negative conceptions.) οὐ μή (intensive), not at all, by no means.

οὐδέ, conj., neither, nor.

οὐδείς, οὐδεμία, οὐδέν, no one, none, not one.

οὐδέποτε, adv., never.

οὖν, conj., therefore, then.

οὔπω, adv., not yet.

οὐράνιος, α, ον, adj., heavenly.

οὐρανός, οῦ, ὁ, heaven.

οὗτος, αὕτη, τοῦτο, this.

οὕτως (by some editors written οὕτω before a consonant), adv., so, thus.

οὐχί (a strengthened form of οὐ), not.

ὀφθαλμός, οῦ, ὁ, an eye.

ὄχλος, ου, ὁ, a crowd, a multitude.

Π.

παιδίον, ου, τό, a little child, a child.

παιδίσκη, ης, ἡ, a maiden, a maid-servant.

παῖς, παιδός, ὁ, ἡ, a boy, a girl, a servant.

πάλιν, adv., again.

παρά (with gen., dat. and acc.), near by, by, beside, from, of.

παραβολή, ῆς, ἡ, a parable.

πᾶς, πᾶσα, πᾶν, adj., all, every.

πάσχω, to suffer.

πατήρ, G. πατρός, ὁ, a father.

Παῦλος, ου, ὁ, Paul.

πεντηκοστή, ῆς, ἡ, Pentecost.

περί (with gen. and acc.), about, concerning.

περιάγω, to lead about, to go about.
περιπατέω, to walk about, to walk.
περισσεύω, to cause to abound.
πετεινόν, οῦ, τό, a fowl, a bird.
πέτρα, as, ἡ, a rock.
Πέτρος, ου, ὁ, Peter.
πινακίδιον, ου, τό, a tablet.
πίναξ, ακος, ὁ, a trencher, plate, platter.
πίπτω, to fall.
πιστεύω, to have faith, to believe, to believe in, to put trust in, to trust, to intrust ; pass., to be believed, to be intrusted with.
πίστις, εως, ἡ, faith.
πλείων, ον, adj. (compar. of πολύς), more, greater.
πληγή, ῆς, ἡ, a plague.
πλῆθος, εος, ους, τό, a great number, a multitude.
πλήρης, ες, adj., full.
πληρόω, to fill, to fulfil.
πλησίον, adv., near ; ὁ πλησίον, a neighbor.
πλοῦς, G. πλοός, ὁ, navigation.
πνεῦμα, ατος, τό, breath, wind, spirit.
ποιέω, to do, to make.
ποιμαίνω, to tend (a flock).
ποιμήν, ένος, ὁ, a herdsman, a shepherd.
ποίμνη, ης, ἡ, a flock.
πόλις, εως, ἡ, a city.
πολλάκις, adv., often.
πολύς, πολλή, πολύ, adj., much, great.
πορεύομαι, to go.
πόσος, η, ον, how great, how much ; pl., how many.
ποτέ, at some time, once, formerly.
ποῦ, adv., where.
πούς, G. πόδος, ὁ, a foot.
πρίν, adv., before.
πρόβατον, ου, τό, a sheep.
προβιβάζω, to urge on.
πρός (with gen., dat. and acc.), to.
προσεύχομαι, to pray (to God).

προσέχω, to take heed.
προσήλυτος, ου, ὁ, ἡ, a proselyte.
προσκυνέω, to worship.
προσφέρω, to bring to, to bring.
πρόσωπον, ου, τό, a face, personal appearance, person.
προφέρω, to bring forth.
προφητεύω, to prophecy.
προφήτης, ου, ὁ, a prophet.
πυνθάνομαι, to ask, to inquire, to learn.
πῦρ, ρός, τό, fire.
πῶς, how.

Σ.

σάββατον, ου, τό, a sabbath.
Σαλαμίς, ῖνος, ἡ, Salamis.
σάρξ, σαρκός, ἡ, flesh.
Σαῦλος, ου, ὁ, Saul.
σεαυτοῦ, of thyself.
σελήνη, ης, ἡ, the moon.
σημεῖον, ου, τό, a sign.
Σιλωάμ, Siloam.
Σίμων, ωνος, ὁ, Simon.
σίναπι, εως, τό, mustard.
σιωπάω, to be silent.
Σολομών, ῶνος, ὁ, Solomon.
σοφία, ας, ἡ, wisdom.
στάχυς, υος, ὁ, an ear of grain.
στόμα, ατος, τό, a mouth.
σύ, thou.
συλλαλέω, to talk with, to converse.
συμφωνέω, to agree with.
σύν (with the dat.), with.
συνάγω, to gather together.
συναγωγή, ῆς, ἡ, a synagogue.
συνέρχομαι, to come together.
συνίημι, to understand.
συσχηματίζω, to conform to.
σφραγίζω, to seal.
σώζω, to heal, to cure, to save.
σῶμα, ατος, τό, a body.

Τ.

ταπεινός, ή, όν, adj., low, lowly, humble.
ταχύς, εῖα, ύ, adj., quick, swift.

τέκνον, ου, τό, a child, a son.
τελώνης, ου, ὁ, a tax-gatherer, a publican.
τετράρχης, ου, ὁ, a tetrarch.
τηρέω, to keep.
τίλλω, to pluck, to pull off.
τιμή, ῆς, ἡ, honor.
τὶς, τὶ, m. f., any one, some one, n. anything, something.
τίς, τί, m. f., who? which? n., what? why? how?
τόπος, ου, ὁ, a place.
τότε, then.
τρεῖς, three.
τρέχω, to run; aor. 2 ἔδραμον.
τρυγάω, to gather (fruit, especially grapes).
τύπτω, to strike.
τυφλός, ή, όν, adj., blind.

Υ.

ὕδωρ, G. ὕδατος, τό, water.
υἱός, οῦ, ὁ, a son.
ὑμεῖς (pl. of σύ), you.
ὑπάγω, to go.
ὑπακούω, to hearken unto.
ὑπέρ (with gen. and acc.), over, because of.
ὑπό (with gen. and acc.), by.
ὑπολαμβάνω, to suppose.
ὑποστρέφω, to turn back, to return.
ὗς, ὑός, ὁ, ἡ, a swine.
ὕψος, ους, τό, elevation, dignity.
ὑψόω, to lift up.

Φ.

φάγος, ου, ὁ, a glutton.
φαίνω, to show; pass. or mid., to appear.
φανός, οῦ, ὁ, a light, a torch, a lantern.
Φαρισαῖος, ου, ὁ, a Pharisee.
φέρω, to bear.
φεύγω, to flee, to escape; aor. 2 ἔφυγον.

φημί, to say.
φιλαδελφία, ας, brotherly love.
φιλέω, to love.
Φίλιππος, ου, ὁ, Philip.
φίλος, ου, ὁ, a friend.
φοβέομαι, to be frightened, to fear, to reverence.
φόβος, ου, ὁ, fear.
φονεύω, to kill.
φρέαρ, φρέατος, τό, a well, a pit.
φρόνιμος, η, ον, adj., prudent, wise.
φυλή, ῆς, ἡ, a tribe.
φυτεία, ας, ἡ, a plant.
φυτεύω, to plant.
φωνή, ῆς, ἡ, a voice.

Χ.

χάλαζα, ης, ἡ, hail.
χείρ, ρός, ἡ, a hand.
χήρα, ας, ἡ, a widow.
χλαμύς, ύδος, a robe, — probably a military cloak.
χοῖρος, ου, ὁ, ἡ, a swine.
χοῦς, οός, ὁ, earth, dirt, dust.
χράομαι, to use, to make use of.
χρεία, ας, ἡ, need.
χριστός, adj., anointed; ὁ Χριστός, the Christ, Christ.
χρόνος, ου, ὁ, time.
χρυσός, οῦ, ὁ, gold.
χωρίς, apart from, besides.

Ψ.

ψαλμός, οῦ, ὁ, a psalm.
ψευδοπροφήτης, ου, ὁ, a false prophet.

Ω.

ὧδε, adv., here.
ᾠδή, ῆς, ἡ, an ode, a song.
ὠδίν, ῖνος, ἡ, a birth-pang.
ὡς, adv., as, as it were.
ὡσεί, as if, about.
ὥσπερ, adv., just as.

APPENDIX.

A. Synopsis of the verb πιστεύω.

ACTIVE VOICE.

	Indicative.	Subjunctive.	Optative.	Imperative.	Infinitive.	Participle.
Pres.	πιστεύω,	πιστεύω	πιστεύοιμι	πίστευε	πιστεύειν	πιστεύων
Imperf.	ἐπίστευον					
Fut.	πιστεύσω				πιστεύσειν	πιστεύσων
Aor.	ἐπίστευσα	πιστεύσω	πιστεύσαιμι	πίστευσον	πιστεῦσαι	πιστεύσας
Perf.	πεπίστευκα				πεπιστευκέναι	πεπιστευκώς
Plup.	ἐπεπιστεύκειν					

PASSIVE AND MIDDLE VOICES.

	Indicative.	Subjunctive.	Optative.	Imperative.	Infinitive.	Participle.
Pres.	πιστεύομαι	πιστεύωμαι	πιστευοίμην	πιστεύου	πιστεύεσθαι	πιστευόμενος
Imperf.	ἐπιστευόμην					
Fut. Mid.	πιστεύσομαι					
Fut. Pass.	πιστευθήσομαι					
Aor. Pass.	ἐπιστεύθην	πιστευθῶ	πιστευθείην	πιστεύθητι	πιστευθῆναι	πιστευθείς
Aor. Mid.	ἐπιστευσάμην	πιστεύσωμαι	πιστευσαίμην	πίστευσαι	πιστεύσασθαι	πιστευσάμενος
Perf.	πεπίστευμαι			πεπίστευσο	πεπιστεῦσθαι	πεπιστευμένος
Plup.	ἐπεπιστεύμην					

B. Paradigm of the verb πιστεύω.*

ACTIVE VOICE. — *Indicative Mode.*

Present.

Sing. 1. πιστεύω
2. πιστεύεις
3. πιστεύει
Pl. 1. πιστεύομεν
2. πιστεύετε
3. πιστεύουσι(ν)

Imperfect.

Sing. 1. [ἐπίστευον]
2. [ἐπίστευες]
3. ἐπίστευε(ν)
Pl. 1. [ἐπιστεύομεν]
2. ἐπιστεύετε
3. ἐπίστευον

Future.

Sing. 1. πιστεύσω
2. [πιστεύσεις]
3. πιστεύσει
Pl. 1. πιστεύσομεν
2. πιστεύσετε
3. πιστεύσουσι(ν)

Aorist.

Sing. 1. ἐπίστευσα
2. ἐπίστευσας
3. ἐπίστευσε(ν)
Pl. 1. ἐπιστεύσαμεν
2. ἐπιστεύσατε
3. ἐπίστευσαν

Perfect.

Sing. 1. πεπίστευκα
2. πεπίστευκας
3. πεπίστευκε(ν)
Pl. 1. πεπιστεύκαμεν
2. πεπιστεύκατε
3. [πεπιστεύκασι(ν)]

Pluperfect.

Sing. 1. [ἐπεπιστεύκειν]
2. [ἐπεπιστεύκεις]
3. [ἐπεπιστεύκει]
Pl. 1. [ἐπεπιστεύκειμεν]
2. [ἐπεπιστεύκειτε]
3. ἐπεπιστεύκεισαν

Subjunctive Mode.

Present.

Sing. 1. [πιστεύω]
2. [πιστεύῃς]
3. πιστεύῃ
Pl. 1. [πιστεύωμεν]
2. πιστεύητε
3. [πιστεύωσι(ν)]

Aorist.

Sing. 1. πιστεύσω
2. πιστεύσῃς
3. πιστεύσῃ
Pl. 1. πιστεύσωμεν
2. πιστεύσητε
3. πιστεύσωσι(ν)

Optative Mode.

Present.

Sing. 1. [πιστεύοιμι]
2. [πιστεύοις]
3. [πιστεύοι]
Pl. 1. [πιστεύοιμεν]
2. [πιστεύοιτε]
3. [πιστεύοιεν]

Aorist.

Sing. 1. [πιστεύσαιμι]
2. [πιστεύσαις]
3. [πιστεύσαι]
Pl. 1. [πιστεύσαιμεν]
2. [πιστεύσαιτε]
3. [πιστεύσαιεν or -ειαν]

* For infinitives and participles, see "Synopsis," p. 61.

Imperative Mode.

Present.
Sing. 2. πίστευε
    3. [πιστευέτω]
Pl. 2. πιστεύετε
    3. [πιστευέτωσαν]

Aorist.
Sing. 2. πίστευσον
    3. [πιστευσάτω]
Pl. 2. πιστεύσατε
    3. [πιστευσάτωσαν]

PASSIVE AND MIDDLE VOICES. — Indicative Mode.

Present passive and middle.
Sing. 1. [πιστεύομαι]
    2. [πιστεύῃ]
    3. πιστεύεται
Pl. 1. [πιστευόμεθα]
    2. [πιστεύεσθε]
    3. [πιστεύονται]

Imperfect passive and middle.
Sing. 1. [ἐπιστευόμην]
    2. [ἐπιστεύου]
    3. [ἐπιστεύετο]
Pl. 1. [ἐπιστευόμεθα]
    2. [ἐπιστεύεσθε]
    3. [ἐπιστεύοντο]

Future passive.
Sing. 1. [πιστευθήσομαι]
    2. [πιστευθήσῃ]
    3. [πιστευθήσεται]
Pl. 1. [πιστευθησόμεθα]
    2. [πιστευθήσεσθε]
    3. [πιστευθήσονται]

Future middle.
Sing. 1. [πιστεύσομαι]
    2. [πιστεύσῃ]
    3. [πιστεύσεται]
Pl. 1. [πιστευσόμεθα]
    2. [πιστεύσεσθε]
    3. [πιστεύσονται]

Aorist passive.
Sing. 1. ἐπιστεύθην
    2. [ἐπιστεύθης]
    3. ἐπιστεύθη
Pl. 1. [ἐπιστεύθημεν]
    2. [ἐπιστεύθητε]
    3. ἐπιστεύθησαν

Aorist middle.
Sing. 1. [ἐπιστευσάμην]
    2. [ἐπιστεύσω]
    3. [ἐπιστεύσατο]
Pl. 1. [ἐπιστευσάμεθα]
    2. [ἐπιστεύσασθε]
    3. [ἐπιστεύσαντο]

Perfect passive and middle.
Sing. 1. πεπίστευμαι
    2. [πεπίστευσαι]
    3. [πεπίστευται]
Pl. 1. [πεπιστεύμεθα]
    2. [πεπίστευσθε]
    3. [πεπίστευνται]

Pluperfect passive and middle.
Sing. 1. [ἐπεπιστεύμην]
    2. [ἐπεπίστευσο]
    3. [ἐπεπίστευτο]
Pl. 1. [ἐπεπιστεύμεθα]
    2. [ἐπεπίστευσθε]
    3. [ἐπεπίστευντο]

Subjunctive Mode.

Present passive and middle.
Sing. 1. [πιστεύωμαι]
    2. [πιστεύῃ]
    3. [πιστεύηται]

Pl. 1. [πιστευώμεθα]
    2. [πιστεύησθε]
    3. [πιστεύωνται]

Aorist passive.

Sing. 1. [πιστευθῶ]
    2. [πιστευθῇς]
    3. [πιστευθῇ]
Pl. 1. [πιστευθῶμεν]
    2. [πιστευθῆτε]
    3. [πιστευθῶσι(ν)]

Aorist middle.

Sing. 1. [πιστεύσωμαι]
    2. [πιστεύσῃ]
    3. [πιστεύσηται]
Pl. 1. [πιστευσώμεθα]
    2. [πιστεύσησθε]
    3. [πιστεύσωνται]

Optative Mode.

Present passive and middle.

Sing. 1. [πιστευοίμην]
    2. [πιστεύοιο]
    3. [πιστεύοιτο]
Pl. 1. [πιστευοίμεθα]
    2. [πιστεύοισθε]
    3. [πιστεύοιντο]

Aorist passive.

Sing. 1. [πιστευθείην]
    2. [πιστευθείης]
    3. [πιστευθείη]
Pl. 1. [πιστευθείημεν]
    2. [πιστευθείητε]
    3. [πιστευθείησαν]

Aorist middle.

Sing. 1. [πιστευσαίμην]
    2. [πιστεύσαιο]
    3. [πιστεύσαιτο]
Pl. 1. [πιστευσαίμεθα]
    2. [πιστεύσαισθε]
    3. [πιστεύσαιντο]

Imperative Mode.

Present passive and middle.

Sing. 2. [πιστεύου]
    3. [πιστευέσθω]
Pl. 2. [πιστεύεσθε]
    3. [πιστευέσθωσαν]

Perfect passive and middle.

Sing. 2. [πεπίστευσο]
    3. [πεπιστεύσθω]
Pl. 2. [πεπίστευσθε]
    3. [πεπιστεύσθωσαν]

Aorist passive.

Sing. 2. [πιστεύθητι]
    3. [πιστευθήτω]
Pl. 2. [πιστεύθητε]
    3. [πιστευθήτωσαν]

Aorist middle.

Sing. 2. [πίστευσαι]
    3. [πιστευσάσθω]
Pl. 2. [πιστεύσασθε]
    3. [πιστευσάσθωσαν]

C. Tabular View of the Endings of Nouns.

		Singular.				Plural.				
	N.	G.	D.	A.	V.	N.	G.	D.	A.	
First Declension. a	ης	ῃ	αν			αι	ων	αις	ας	§§ 8, 10, 12, 14; 15, 17.
η	ης	ῃ	ην			αι	ων	αις	ας	
a	ας	ᾳ	αν			αι	ων	αις	ας	
ας	ου	ᾳ	αν			αι	ων	αις	ας	
ης	ου (η)	ῃ	ην	a		αι	ων	αις	ας	
ας	a	ᾳ	αν	a		αι	ων	αις	ας	
Second Declension. ος	ου	ῳ	ον	ε		οι	ων	οις	ους	§ 19
ον	ου	ῳ	ον			a	ων	οις	a	"
Third Declension. a	ατος	ατι	a			ατα	ατων	ασιν	ατα	§ 22
αρ	ατος		αρ							"
ας	ατος	ατι	ας			ατα	ατων	ασιν	ατα	"
υ	[ατος]		υ					ασιν	ατα	"
ωρ	ατος	ατι	ωρ			ατα	ατων	ασιν	ατα	"
αις	αιδος		αιδα				αιδων	αισιν	αιδας	§ 24
ας	αδος	αδι	αδα			αδες	αδων	ασιν	αδας	"
εις	ειδος	ειδι	ειδα			ειδες	ειδων	εισιν	ειδας	"
ις	ιδος	ιδι	ιδα			ιδες	ιδων	ισιν	ιδας	"
ους	οδος		οδα			οδες	οδων	οσιν	οδας	"
υς	υδος	υδι	υδα			υδες	υδων	υσιν	υδας	"
ις	[ιθος]									"
ης	ητος	ητι	ητα			ητες	ητων	ησιν	ητας	§ 25
ι	[ιτος]		ι							"
ις	ιτος	ιτι	ιτα			ιτες	ιτων	ισιν	ιτας	"
ως	ωτος	ωτι	ως				ωτων			"
ους	[ωτος]		ους			ωτα		ωσιν	ωτα	"
ξ	κος	κι	κα			κες	κων	ξιν	κας	§ 27
ξ	γος	γι	γα			γες	γων	ξιν	γας	"
ξ	χος	χι	χα			χες	χων	ξιν	χας	"
ξ	κτος	κτι	κτα			κτες	κτων	ξιν	κτας	"
ψ	πος	πι	πα			πες	πων	ψιν	πας	"
ψ	βος	βι	βα			βες	βων	ψιν	βας	"
η	αικος	αικι	αικα	αι		αικες	αικων	αιξιν	αικας	"
[a]	ακτος		a							"
ας	αντος	αντι	αντα			αντες	αντων	ασιν	αντας	§ 29
ης	εντος									"

	Singular					Plural				
Third Declension, continued.	N.	G.	D.	A.	V.	N.	G.	D.	A.	
	ους	οντος		οντα		οντες	οντων		οντας	§ 29
	ων	οντος	οντι	-οντα		οντες	οντων	ουσιν	οντας	"
	[αυς]			αυν						§ 31
	ευς	εως	ει	εα	ευ	εις	εων	ευσιν	εις	"
	ης	εως	ει	εα						"
			(η)	(ην)						"
	[ι]	εως								"
	ις	εως	ει	ιν		εις	εων	εσιν	εις	"
	υς	εως		υν			ων			"
							(εων)			"
	αρ	αρος	αρι	αρα		αρες	αρων	αρσιν	αρας	§ 33
	ειρ	ειρος	ειρι	ειρα		ειρες	ειρων	ερσιν	ειρας	"
	ηρ	ηρος	ηρι	ηρα		ηρες	ηρων	ηρσιν	ηρας	"
	ηρ	ερος	ερι	ερα		ερες	ερων	ερσιν	ερας	"
	υρ	υρος	υρι	υρ						"
	υς	υρος		υρα		υρες	υρων	υσιν	υρας	"
	ωρ	ορος	ορι	ορα		ορες	ορων	ορσιν	ορας	"
	ηρ	ρος	ρι	ερα	ερ	ερες	ερων	ρασιν	ερας	§ 35
	ηρ	δρος	δρι	δρα	ερ	δρες	δρων	δρασιν	δρας	"
	ην	ηνος	ηνι	ηνα		ηνες	ηνων	ησιν	ηνας	§ 37
	ην	ενος	ενι	ενα		ενες	ενων	εσιν	ενας	"
	ιν						ινων		ινας	"
	[ις]		ινι							"
	ων	ωνος	ωνι	ωνα		ωνες	ωνων	ωσιν	ωνας	"
	ων	ονος	ονι	ονα		ονες	ονων	οσιν	ονας	"
	ος	ους	ει	ος		η	ων	εσιν	η	§ 39
							(εων)			"
	[ως]	ους								"
	ους			ουν			οων		οας	§ 40
	υ	υος	υι	υ		υα	υων	υσιν	υα	§ 42
	υς	υος	υι	υν		υες	υων	υσιν	υας	"

COMMENTARIES

PUBLISHED BY

WARREN F. DRAPER,

ANDOVER, MASS.

These Books will be sent, post-paid, on receipt of the price affixed.

Ellicott. *Commentaries, Critical and Grammatical, by C. J. Ellicott, Bishop of Gloucester and Bristol, viz. on*

GALATIANS. With an Introductory Notice by C. E. STOWE, lately
Professor in Andover Theological Seminary. 8vo. pp. 183. $1.50
EPHESIANS. 8vo. pp. 190.   1.50
THESSALONIANS. 8vo. pp. 171.   1.50
THE PASTORAL EPISTLES. 8vo. pp. 265.   2.00
PHILIPPIANS, COLOSSIANS, and PHILEMON. 8vo. pp. 265. 2.00
    THE SET in five volumes, tinted paper, bevelled edges, gilt tops,
    THE SET in two volumes, black cloth, bevelled edges,   8.00

"We would recommend all scholars of the original Scriptures who
seek directness, luminous brevity, the absence of everything irrelevant to
strict grammatical inquiry, with a concise and yet very complete view of
the opinions of others, to possess themselves of Ellicott's Commentaries."
— *American Presbyterian.*

"His Commentaries are among the best, if not the very best, helps a
student can have." — *American Presbyterian and Theological Review.*

"Ellicott is one of the best commentators of this class."—*Princeton Rev.*

"I do not know of anything superior to them in their own particular
line." — *Dean Alford.*

**Hackett. A Commentary on the Original Text of the
* Acts of the Apostles.** By HORATIO B. HACKETT, D.D.,
Professor of Biblical Literature in Newton Theological
Institution. A new edition, revised and greatly enlarged.
8vo. Cloth, $3.50

This is a reprint of the last edition revised by Prof. Hackett himself.

Lightfoot. St. Paul's Epistle to the Galatians. A Revised
Text, with Introduction, Notes, and Dissertations. By
J. B. LIGHTFOOT, D.D., Hulsean Professor of Divinity,
and Fellow of Trinity College Cambridge. 8vo. pp. 402.
Bevelled edges, $3.00

"Taken as a whole, we venture to say that this is the most complete
and exhaustive Commentary on the Epistle to the Galatians that has yet
appeared, Ellicott's not excepted." — *Christian Intelligencer.*

Henderson. *Commentaries, Critical, Philological, and Exegetical, viz. on*

The Book of the Twelve Minor Prophets. Translated from the Original Hebrew. By E. HENDERSON, D.D. With a Biographical Sketch of the Author, by E. P. BARROWS, Hitchcock Professor in Andover Theol. Sem. 8vo. $3.50

"The work is invaluable for its philological research and critical acumen. . . . . . The notes are learned, reliable, and practical." —*American Presbyterian, etc.*

" This is probably the best commentary extant on the Minor Prophets." —*Christian Chronicle.*

"It is altogether the best commentary in existence on the Minor Prophets." —*Religious Union.*

"The Minor Prophets is a valuable book. Dr. Henderson is very careful to avoid fanciful interpretations — at least this is his canon, and there is much good sense shown everywhere." —*Presbyterian Quarterly.*

" We have met with no so satisfactory a commentary on this part of the prophetic Scripture." — *Watchman and Reflector.*

"The only satisfactory commentary on the Minor Prophets we know of in the English language." —*Episcopal Recorder.*

"Dr. Henderson's commentaries are rich in wholesome and true exposition." —*Presbyterian Magazine.*

"The notes are replete with the fruits of varied learning." —*The Presbyterian.*

Jeremiah and Lamentations. Translated from the original Hebrew. 8vo. $2.50

" Whatever surrounds the reader with the national life of the Hebrews enables him to understand the sacred writers. In addition, the critical student needs exegetical helps in catching the sense of the author. Dr. Henderson has undertaken to meet these wants to a considerable extent, and has succeeded well. Those ministers who are in the habit of giving brief expositions of the prophetic writing will find great assistance from this volume." —*Congregational Review.*

" It is a scholarly and devout analysis of the saddest of the prophets. It is a valuable contribution to our biblical literature " —*Zion's Herald*

"This admirable commentary meets a want long felt by biblical students. Those acquainted with Dr. Henderson's work on the Minor Prophets need scarcely be told of the ability and learning and piety which characterize this volume." —*Protestant Churchman.*

Ezekiel. Translated from the original Hebrew. 8vo. pp. 228. Cloth, $2.00

" The same diligence, learning, sobriety, and judiciousness characterize it as the learned author's commentaries on Isaiah, Jeremiah, and the Minor Prophets." — *Bibliotheca Sacra.*

"He is throughout reverent and modest, yet scholarly and wonderfully clear. . . . . . We know of no better interpreter of Ezekiel than Dr. Henderson." — *Watchman and Reflector.*

Books Published by W. F. Draper.

Murphy. Critical and Exegetical Commentaries by Prof. James G. Murphy, LL.D., T.C.D., viz.

Genesis. With a New Translation. With a Preface by J. P. THOMPSON, D.D., New York. 8vo. pp. 535. $3.50

"The most valuable contribution that has for a long time been made to the many aids for the critical study of the Old Testament is Mr. Draper's republication of Dr. Murphy on Genesis, in one octavo volume. Dr. Murphy is one of the Professors of the Assembly's College at Belfast, and adds to a thorough knowledge of the Hebrew, and of the science of interpretation, great common sense, genuine wit, and admirable power of expression. Hence his Commentary is racy and readable, as well as reliable. No volume will be more useful to those who have been troubled by the Colenso criticisms ; and no man has pricked the bubble of that inflated bishop with a more effectual and relieving wound than Dr.Murphy." — *Congregationalist.*

"Dr. Murphy is a fair, clear,. and candid interpreter. His aim is to reconcile the Scriptures with science by an impartial examination of the text." —*American Presbyterian and Theological Review.*

Exodus. With a New Translation. 8vo. pp. 385. $3.00

"Thus far nothing has appeared in this country for half a century on the first two books of the Pentateuch so valuable as the present two volumes." [On Genesis and Exodus]. "His style is lucid, animated, and often eloquent. His pages afford golden suggestions and key-thoughts. ..... Some of the laws of interpretation are stated with so fresh and natural a clearness and force that they will permanently stand."—*Methodist Quarterly.*

"Prof. Murphy's Commentary on Genesis has been published long enough to have secured the highest reputation for scholarship, research, and sound judgment. This volume on Exodus takes its place in the same rank, and will increase rather than diminish its author's reputation among scholars." — *National Baptist.*

"By its originality and critical accuracy it must command the high regard of the scholar and theologian, whilst the ease and grace of its style, the judiciousness with which it selects and unfolds its many subjects of discussion, will be sure to fix and reward the attention of the general student." — *The Lutheran.*

Leviticus. With a New Translation. 8vo. pp. 318. $2.50

"In our opinion, his idea and method are the right one, and the whole work shows a remarkably clear mastery of the subject. His style, too, is singularly lucid. He interprets Hebrew well, and writes capital English. The book meets a long-felt want, and meets it well."—*The Advance.*

"The obscure and difficult portions of the text are elucidated with great skill and impressiveness, and the whole work furnishes a most interesting study."—*The Lutheran and Missionary.*

"The Commentaries of Murphy have many excellences. They are clear, discriminating, and comprehensive." — *Baptist Quarterly.*

"We think it is the very best Commentary on Leviticus that has ever been published." — *The Presbyterian.*

"We know of no work on Leviticus comparable with it." — *Pulpit and Pew.*

Psalms. With a new Translation. By J. G. Murphy, $4.00

" This Commentary is well fitted to meet the wants of pastors in preparing their expositions of the Psalms. The more educated teachers of Bible-classes and Sabbath-schools may study it with advantage. They need not be deterred from using it by the presence of the Hebrew words which are conspicuous on some of its pages. Like the other Commentaries of Dr. Murphy, this is distinguished by the ease and perspicuity of its style, its freedom from pedantry, and the excellent religious spirit pervading it. The Introduction, occupying the first fifty pages, is lucid and interesting." — *Bibliothecu Sacru.*

" It is on the whole one of the best expositions of the Psalms accessible for popular instruction, and a valuable auxiliary to the work of preachers and teachers." — *Examiner and Chronicle.*

Perowne. **The Book of Psalms;** a New Translation. With Introductions and Notes Explanatory and Critical. By J. J. STEWART PEROWNE, D.D., Fellow of Trinity College, Cambridge, and Canon of Llandaff. Reprinted from the Third English Edition. In Two Volumes. 8vo. $7.50

" It comprises in itself more excellences than any other commentary on the Psalms in our language, and we know of no single commentary in the German language which, all things considered, is preferable to it." — *Baptist Quarterly.*

" Very rare, indeed, is it that such a combination of requisites to a just exposition of Scripture, and particularly of this portion of Scripture, are combined in one work, — such scholarship, such judgment, such taste, such spiritual insight, such wisdom in the general treatment of his subject, such skill as a translator, such simplicity and sustained vigor of style." — *The Advance.*

" This is justly regarded as the standard commentary on the Book of Psalms in England. It is learned, devout, and exhaustive. . . . . Dr. Perowne is one of the most profound Hebrew scholars in Europe, and his translation of the Hebrew text gives abundant evidence of his learning." — *Lutheran Observer.*

" The Introductions combine a series of able essays upon the structure, history, literature, and theology of the Psalms. The new translation adheres closely to the Hebrew original. The critical notes evince great biblical learning, rigid fidelity in the use of the Hebrew dictionary and grammar, and a reigning principle of arriving at the exact meaning of every word, rather than to give an elegant or metrical style to the rendering. Its practical reflections are select and pointed. Dr. Perowne does not evade difficulties, as do some commentators, and where his conclusions are not satisfactory to the student, he will, at least, have the assurance of honest dealing with the embarrassments of all interpreters." — *Christian Intelligencer.*

" If there is a better exposition of the Psalms in the English language we do not know what it is. The Introduction and Notes are models in their kind. Probably no one in England is more capable than Professor Perowne of doing all that Hebrew scholarship can do towards a better knowledge of the Psalms." — *The Contributor.*

Books Published by W. F. Draper.

An Examination of the Alleged Discrepancies of the Bible. By John W. Haley, M.A. With an Introduction by Alvah Hovey, D.D., Professor in the Newton Theological Institution. Crown 8vo. pp. xii and 473. $2.00

"I do not know any volume which gives to the English reader such a compressed amount of suggestion and instruction on this theme as is given in this volume."—*Prof. Edwards A. Park.*

"A book so costly in great qualities, yet so cheap and accessible to all; one so scholarly and yet so simple and usable; one so creditable to its author, and yet so modestly sent forth, does not every day appear. As an example of thorough and painstaking scholarship, as a serviceable hand-book for all Bible students, and as a popular defence of revealed truth, it will take high rank, and fill an important place which up to this time has been conspicuously vacant." — *Congregationalist.*

A Statement of the Natural Sources of Theology; with a Discussion of their Validity, and of Modern Sceptical Objections; to which is added an Article on the First Chapter of Genesis. By Thomas Hill, D.D., LL.D. Reprinted from the Bibliotheca Sacra. 8vo. pp. 144. Paper, 60 cts.; Cloth, flexible, 80 cents·

CONTENTS. — Theology a Possible Science. — The Foundations of Theology sure. — The Natural Foundations of Theology. — The Testimony of Organic Life. — The Natural Sources of Theology. — The First Chapter of Genesis.

"Powerful discussions, rich in thought and illustration, and directed with crushing force against the positions of infidel scientists."—*Advance.*
" A masterly series of articles." — *National Baptist.*

Hermeneutics of the New Testament. By Dr. A. Immer, Professor of Theology in the University of Berne. Translated from the German by Rev. Albert H. Newman. With additional Notes and full Indexes. Crown 8vo. pp. 413. $2.25

"It is a thoroughly scientific and almost exhaustive treatise on the whole subject. It is in three parts: I. The General Principles of Hermeneutics; II. The Single Operations of the Scripture Interpreter; III. The Religious Understanding. The elaborate history of Scripture interpretation and the several methods of exegesis that have from time to time been employed, constitute a very important portion of the work. ... We heartily commend it to our young ministers in particular, in the belief that in mastering it they will greatly enrich their teachings of the sacred word." — *Methodist Quarterly Review.*

"Perfect in method, thorough, and truly German in its scholarship, yet fresh and interesting in its treatment, and translated in a clear and attractive English style, it will meet a real need of theological students and ministers, and must stimulate a scholarly study on the part of such."
—*Christian Register.*   1–78